The Giant Book of Wacky Facts

I0787816

By
Jake Jacobs

Kindle Edition

* * * * *

Published by Jake Jacobs at Amazon Kindle

The Giant Book of Wacky Facts
Copyright© 2018 by Jake Jacobs

1.

Venus spins in the opposite direction of Earth.

Reference: (http://solarsystem.nasa.gov/planets/venus/basic#!)

2.

Neanderthals' voices were actually high-pitched and nasal, not deep and baritone like many assume.

Reference: (http://www.mentalfloss.com/article.php?id=19428)

3.

In 1944, Karl Leisner secretly became the only Catholic priest to be ordained while imprisoned in a Nazi concentration camp.

Reference: (http://www.catholictradition.org/Priests/dachau.htm)

4.

A man died, came back to life and won the lottery twice. The second time he won, he was reenacting the first win for the media.

Reference:
(http://edition.cnn.com/WORLD/asiapcf/9905/27/fringe/australia.luckiest.man/)

5.

Bergen County, New Jersey, has "Blue Laws" that ban shopping on Sundays.

Reference: (http://www.newyorker.com/business/currency/americas-last-ban-sunday-shopping)

6.

Koko the Gorilla was a fan of Mr. Rogers and got to meet him.

Reference: (https://www.youtube.com/watch?v=cn79Lgfh1hw)

7.

Sherlock Holmes is the most portrayed movie character in history.

Reference: (https://en.wikipedia.org/wiki/Sherlock_Holmes#cite_note-:0-1)

8.

The Mexican silver dollar became the dominant currency of southern and eastern China in the 1830s.

Reference: (http://w3.unisa.edu.au/unisanews/2014/September/story11.asp)

9.

The head coach of the San Antonio Spurs benched superstar Tim Duncan, listing the reasoning as "old."

Reference: (http://sports.yahoo.com/blogs/nba-ball-dont-lie/tim-duncan-missed-sunday-night-spurs-game-because-081218158.html)

10.

The Mexican party scene has fully embraced ridiculously long and pointy boots. Known as "botas picudas", the Mexican fashion of pointy boots started with tribal music. In the beginning, people were using regular boots then they started making them pointer and pointer, until it got out of control.

Reference: (https://www.youtube.com/watch?v=veQkt4tS0Tc)

11.

Snails use just two brain cells to make decisions.

Reference: (http://www.lbc.co.uk/snails-use-just-two-brain-cells-to-make-decisions-131640)

12.

People in England can be ordered to tell police 24 hours before they plan to have sex or face jail, even if they have never been convicted of any crime.

Reference: (http://www.bbc.com/news/uk-england-york-north-yorkshire-35385227)

13.

There are giant earthworms in Washington that have gone from extinct to having a massive population.

Reference:
(http://www.npr.org/templates/story/story.php?storyId=126312580)

14.

The state of Arizona doesn't observe Daylight Savings Time.

Reference:
(http://www.usatoday.com/story/news/nation/2015/03/08/no-arizona-daylight-saving-time/24619125/)

15.

3 of the 3 sunk U.S. battleships at the Attack on Pearl Harbor were later raised, returned to service, and used to fight in World War II.

Reference: (https://en.wikipedia.org/wiki/Attack_on_Pearl_Harbor)

16.

The term "Internet Cookies" traces back to fortune cookies, as they contain messages.

Reference:
(https://en.wikipedia.org/wiki/HTTP_cookie#Origin_of_the_name)

17.

The illusionist, David Copperfield, once used sleight of hand to trick his would be robbers in to thinking he had nothing to steal.

Reference:
(https://en.wikipedia.org/wiki/David_Copperfield_(illusionist)#Personal_life)

18.

The word "mortgage" means "death pledge" in Old French.

Reference: (http://www.msn.com/en-us/money/realestate/10-reasons-you-should-retire-to-a-tiny-house/ss-BBsmN9x#image=2)

19.

It's the aging of the cigar wrapper that makes it dark, not just the strain of tobacco.

Reference: (http://www.cigarsinternational.com/cigar-101/article/11/cigar-wrappers)

20.

When Lyndon B. Johnson left office, he advised Richard Nixon to always have recorded phone conversations in the Oval Office.

Reference: (http://thedailyshow.cc.com/episodes/m8wxgw/july-29--2015---doris-kearns-goodwin)

21.

An artist is trying to spread awareness of bee health by personally painting 50,000 bees in murals across the United States.

Reference: (http://www.thegoodofthehive.com/about/)

22.

There is an international policy on how to deal with incoming messages from extraterrestrial civilizations.

Reference: (https://en.wikipedia.org/wiki/Post-detection_policy)

23.

In 2012, during a protest of the use of fracking in Culver City, Michael Myers showed up to show his love and support for fracking.

Reference:
(http://latimesblogs.latimes.com/lanow/2012/06/protesters-take-to-culver-city-streets-to-decry-fracking-.html)

24.

On April 6th, 1893, Andy Bowen and Jack Burke were involved in the longest boxing fight in history. The fight lasted 111 rounds, at 3 minute rounds each. It took 7 hours and 19 minutes until referee John Duffy called "no contest" after both men were too dazed and tired to come out of their corners.

Reference: (https://en.wikipedia.org/wiki/Andy_Bowen)

25.

Shaving your legs makes you faster on a bicycle. More specifically, it makes you a full 15 watts faster at race pace.

Reference: (http://online.wsj.com/articles/how-to-shave-off-a-few-seconds-1412204666)

26.

The 1st draft of Anchorman was about a planeload of news anchors who crash in the mountains, the men soon discovered the plane they collided with was carrying monkeys and martial arts gear, leading to a battle-to-the-death between cannibalistic anchors and star-throwing monkeys.

Reference: (https://oneroomwithaview.com/2013/05/08/50-slices-of-movie-trivia-you-may-not-know/?xx)

27.

Japanese paratroopers in World War II had rifles that folded in half. They quickly discovered that these modifications didn't work too well.

Reference:
(http://www.popularmechanics.com/military/weapons/a18941/forgot ten-weapons-japans-wwii-paratrooping-rifle/)

28.

Sex alleviates headaches so effectively that some people have started to sex as a treatment for headaches.

Reference: (http://www.redorbit.com/news/health/1112798056/sex-cures-headaches-030513/)

29.

A Town in Poland banned Winnie the Pooh because he doesn't wear pants and they considered him a hermaphrodite.

Reference: (http://www.pinknews.co.uk/2014/11/22/winnie-the-pooh-banned-in-poland-over-dubious-sexuality/)

30.

Germany has a monument to the unknown deserter, honoring soldiers who refused to kill others.

Reference: (http://www.waymarking.com/waymarks/WM2110)

31.

John F. Kennedy criticized the Indian annexation of Portuguese Goa by saying, "You spend the last fifteen years preaching morality to us, and then you go ahead and act the way any normal country would behave. People are saying, the preacher has been caught coming out of the brothel."

Reference:
(https://en.wikipedia.org/wiki/Annexation_of_Portuguese_India#Condemnation)

32.

The Dogon tribe allegedly possess advanced astronomical knowledge, despite the lack of observational equipment.

Reference:
(https://en.wikipedia.org/wiki/Dogon_people#Dogon_and_Sirius)

33.

There's a rule in soccer that says if a player kicks the ball into his own goal on a direct free-kick, the opposing team is awarded a corner kick and not a goal.

Reference:
(https://en.wikipedia.org/wiki/Direct_free_kick#Procedure)

34.

Some people have "blindsight." This means that they are blind due to damage in the brain's visual cortex, but the eye and optic nerve are fine. They can't consciously see anything but can guess their way through an obstacle course or guess the emotional content of a photo through intuition with decent accuracy.

Reference: (https://en.wikipedia.org/wiki/Blindsight)

35.

Students in Karasjok, Norway, don't get to stay home from school until it's -50 degrees Celsius. However, the school bus stops driving when it's -38 degrees Celsius.

Reference:
(https://translate.google.no/translate?sl=no&tl=en&js=y&prev=_t&hl=no&ie=UTF-8&u=http%3A%2F%2Fwww.nrk.no%2Fsapmi%2Fblir-det-kaldere-enn---50_-kan-elevene-holde-seg-hjemme-1.12145152&edit-text=)

36.

Air New Zealand was once hijacked by a man with dynamite who was eventfully thwarted by an engineer who knocked him out with a bottle of whisky and the hijacker now regularly flies with them.

Reference: (http://i.stuff.co.nz/national/10054582/Air-NZ-hijacker-now-flies-with-them)

37.

The only complete and intact work of literature that still exists by a woman in the entire 1200 year history of Greek and Roman antiquity was written by a black woman named Vivia Perpetua.

Reference: (http://www.catholic.org/saints/saint.php?saint_id=48)

38.

"Atuk" is an unfinished film said to be cursed due to the untimely deaths of its four lead actors. These actors were John Belushi, Sam Kinison, John Candy, and Chris Farley.

Reference: (http://www.blumhouse.com/2015/11/23/atuk-the-cursed-screenplay-that-killed-john-belushi-chris-farley-and-more/)

39.

In 2006, a drug trial nearly killed all the participants.

Reference: (https://en.wikipedia.org/wiki/TGN1412)

40.

There's a mountain in Australia called Mt. Disappointment. It was named such because the explorers who first reached its summit found the view to be subpar and wanted to reflect their feelings in the name they chose for the mountain.

Reference:
(https://en.wikipedia.org/wiki/Mount_Disappointment_%28Australia%29)

41.

Between 1959 and 1984, London, Ontario, contained the largest concentration of serial killers in the world.

Reference: (https://en.wikipedia.org/wiki/London,_Ontario)

42.

Cows milked by robots produce significantly higher yields than those milked by hand.

Reference: (http://www.ncbi.nlm.nih.gov/pubmed/12741576)

43.

The common rating scale used in questionnaires asking our responses is called the "Likert Scale".

Reference:
(https://en.wikipedia.org/wiki/Likert_scale#Visual_presentation_of_Likert-type_data)

44.

Bradley Cooper speaks fluent French.

Reference: (https://www.youtube.com/watch?v=2U9TlvTh0GI)

45.

The odds of being dealt a Royal Flush in Poker is 1 in 649,739 or 0.000154%.

Reference: (https://en.wikipedia.org/wiki/Poker_probability)

46.

One man broke into the Buckingham Palace twice.

Reference:(https://www.youtube.com/watch?v=1ljCpjIAW4w&feature=share&list=UURlICXvO4XR4HMeEB9JjDlA&index=3)

47.

On June 9th, 1978, the Mormon Church ended its 148-year-old ban on black people entering the priesthood.

Reference: (http://www.politico.com/story/2007/12/mitt-wept-when-church-ended-discrimination-007415)

48.

Netflix employs "Juicers" to watch movies and shows and pick still images from them that will make you want to watch them.

Reference: (http://www.hollywoodreporter.com/thr-esq/meet-netflixs-juicers-people-who-902730?utm_source=twitter)

49.

Film composer Ennio Morricone got his inspiration of the iconic "The Good, The Bad, and The Ugly" theme from the coyote howl heard at the very beginning of the movie.

Reference: (http://www.filmmusicnotes.com/where-do-film-composers-get-their-ideas-2/)

50.

The Subaru WRX is one of America's most ticketed cars. A recent study done by Insurance.com found that one third of all WRX owners reported receiving a ticket recently.

Reference: (http://www.insurance.com/auto-insurance/vehicle-shopping/cars-that-get-the-most-tickets.html)

51.

A study found a correlation between toxoplasmosis and the risk of being involved in a car accident.

Reference: (http://www.ncbi.nlm.nih.gov/pmc/articles/PMC117239/)

52.

Weird Al Yankovic, Ice-T, Felicia Day, Sean Astin, Wil Wheaton, and several others narrated an audiobook about Dungeons & Dragons character, Drizzt Do'Urden.

Reference: (http://nerdist.com/dungeons-dragons-audiobook-featuring-ice-t-felicia-day-and-more-available-for-free/)

53.

Australia has 31% of the world's uranium supply.

Reference: (http://www.minerals.org.au/resources/uranium/)

54.

There's an increase in time wasting searches the day after Daylight Savings Time starts and people aren't doing anything at work.

Reference: (http://www.rawstory.com/2015/03/how-daylight-savings-time-impacts-your-health/)

55.

One quarter of the world's 2 billion Christians are "Pentecostals or Charismatic Christians", who believe in modern day miracles, signs and wonders, such as speaking in tongues.

Reference: (https://en.wikipedia.org/wiki/Charismatic_Christianity)

56.

Cat urine glows under a black light and the bacteria that causes this effect can remain for years, even after the urine has dried.

Reference: (https://www.catfactstexts.com/cat-facts.html?dd)

57.

Georgia, the country, has lower crime and higher safety indexes than any European state.

Reference:
(http://www.numbeo.com/crime/rankings_by_country.jsp)

58.

Roald Dahl hated beards.

Reference:
(http://www.express.co.uk/entertainment/books/604802/Why-Roald-Dahl-thought-beards-were-Twits)

59.

Silicon Valley uses their own cognitive enhancing drugs called Nootropics that are said to increase short-term memory.

Reference: (http://fusion.net/story/58131/i-tried-silicon-valleys-favorite-brain-enhancing-drugs/)

60.

A former Khmer Rouge member in Cambodia named Aki Ra has been spending the last 20 years disarming landmines all over the country, with no pay and no armor.

Reference: (https://www.youtube.com/watch?v=7Pw-2yMC5BE)

61.

The EPA has approved the use of beer hops to help save the bee population in the United States and stop Colony Collapse Disorder.

Reference: (http://learn.kegerator.com/hops-help-bees/)

62.

Emoticons have been around as early as 1881, first appearing on Puck Magazine.

Reference: (http://www.huffingtonpost.co.uk/2013/07/17/emoticons-first-appeared-1881-puck_n_3609236.html)

63.

The 1977 film "Sorcerer" destroyed the director's career. Unfortunately for him and the studio, it was released one month after "Star Wars". "Sorcerer" was such a box office bomb that it was quickly withdrawn from theaters so that "Star Wars" could return.

Reference:
(https://en.wikipedia.org/wiki/Sorcerer_(film)#Box_office)

64.

Ohio has the highest industrial air pollution in the United States.

Reference: (http://www.worldatlas.com/articles/top-20-most-polluted-states-in-the-us.html)

65.

In a German village called Fuggerei, the rent hasn't been raised since 1520. It costs only 88 cents to live there for an entire year.

Reference: (http://www.wsj.com/articles/SB123025158419834413)

66.

To remove all religious and royalist symbols from society, the French created their own calendar called the Republican Calendar, it was based on the positions of stars and planets and was the official calendar for over 12 years from 1794.

Reference:
(https://en.wikipedia.org/wiki/French_Republican_Calendar)

67.

Violet Jessop survived the sinking of Titanic, its sister ship Britannic and the collision of a third sister ship called Olympic.

Reference: (https://en.wikipedia.org/wiki/Violet_Jessop)

68.

The town with the highest concentration of Icelanders outside of Iceland is called Gimli and is situated in Manitoba, Canada.

Reference: (https://en.wikipedia.org/wiki/Icelanders)

69.

A San Diego park's monorail was named the WGASA Rail Line after managers requested an African sounding name. WGASA is actually an acronym for, "Who Gives A Shit Anyway?"

Reference: (http://www.voiceofsandiego.org/all-narratives/fact/fact-check-wild-animal-parks-naughty-line/)

70.

Pirated copies of the video game "Sims 4" have permanently pixilated Sims, as if they were nude.

Reference: (http://kotaku.com/anyone-who-pirates-the-sims-4-is-in-for-a-surprise-1630684015)

71.

Multiple scientific studies have been conducted to determine if cow-tipping is theoretically possible. All agree that cows are large animals that are difficult to surprise and will generally resist. Estimates suggest that as many as fourteen people would be required to tip a single cow.

Reference: (https://en.wikipedia.org/wiki/Cow_tipping)

72.

Growing use of the internet weakens capacity for abstract vocabulary, mindfulness, reflection, inductive problem solving, critical thinking, and imagination.

Reference: (http://science.sciencemag.org/content/323/5910/69)

73.

William Shatner is a trained Shakespearean stage actor. He was once considered an equal to Steve McQueen, Paul Newman, and Robert Redford, but hurt his career by taking any offered role regardless of quality. That contributed to Shatner joining a no-name cast for "Star Trek" in 1966.

Reference:
(http://www.nytimes.com/2010/09/05/magazine/05Shatner-t.html)

74.

The Corolla Spider uses quartz crystals to set traps and catch its prey.

Reference:
(https://www.youtube.com/watch?v=LhoRAjUBttM&feature=youtu.
be)

75.

On August 27, 1883, a sound emerged from the eruption of the volcanic island of Krakatoa. The sound was heard by people in over 50 different geographical location and spanned an area that covered a thirteenth of the globe. Some people even reported hearing the sound over 3,000 miles away, four hours after the sound was made. A ship's captain even noted in his log that, "so violent are the explosions that the ear-drums of over half my crew have been shattered ... I am convinced that the Day of Judgment has come."

Reference: (http://nautil.us/blog/the-sound-so-loud-that-it-circled-the-earth-four-times)

76.

British people call paper towels "kitchen rolls".

Reference:
(http://dictionary.cambridge.org/us/dictionary/english/kitchen-roll)

77.

Miranda Cosgrove made $180,000 dollars per episode of iCarly, making her the second highest paid child actor on TV.

Reference: (http://www.newser.com/story/88291/tvs-highest-paid-kiddie-actors.html)

78.

Even though Hawaii was never under British rule, it incorporated the union jack into its flag as a symbol of friendship.

Reference: (http://www.bbc.co.uk/news/magazine-35890670)

79.

The inventor of the windshield wiper, Mary Anderson, was granted a patent for it in 1903, she tried to sell the rights in 1905 and was told that it held no commercial value and was unable to sell it. 19 years later, they became standard equipment on every vehicle.

Reference:
(https://en.wikipedia.org/wiki/Mary_Anderson_(inventor))

80.

The Iraqi army was disbanded by the American led coalition in 2003.

Reference:
(http://en.wikipedia.org/wiki/Coalition_Provisional_Authority_Order_2)

81.

Americans call football "soccer" because that's what the British originally called it. The term "soccer" didn't fall out of favor in the United Kingdom till the 1980s.

Reference:
(http://www.theatlantic.com/international/archive/2014/06/why-we-call-soccer-soccer/372771/?mwh=1)

82.

Bullet ants are the second biggest ant on the planet. Each worker ant can reach 18 to 30 millimeters in length.

Reference: (https://www.youtube.com/watch?v=wNCD3rLbCBk)

83.

There is no evidence that people are preferentially "Left Brained" or "Right Brained." Though the brain is divided down the middle into two hemispheres, everything analytical isn't confined to one side of the brain, and everything to do with being creative the opposite.

Reference: (http://www.livescience.com/39373-left-brain-right-brain-myth.html)

84.

If we detonated a hydrogen bomb containing all the deuterium in all the water on Earth, the blast would be powerful enough to create a black hole.

Reference:
(https://en.wikipedia.org/wiki/Micro_black_hole#Manmade_micro_black_holes)

85.

If you're selling property in California and if someone's died on it within the past 3 years, it's considered a material defect and must be disclosed by the seller; that is unless the death was due to AIDS because that's discrimination.

Reference: (http://homeguides.sfgate.com/laws-regarding-death-disclosures-real-estate-transactions-california-46748.html)

86.

The Colossus of Rhodes could have never been built as it is commonly depicted, straddling the harbor of Rhodes, as the statue would have collapsed under its own weight if the legs were placed like that.

Reference:
(https://en.wikipedia.org/wiki/Colossus_of_Rhodes#Posture)

87.

British people call erasers "rubbers" because you can "rub out" mistakes.

Reference: (http://dictionary.cambridge.org/dictionary/english/rub-sth-out)

88.

During the Battle of the Bulge, American MPs trying to uncover German infiltrators would ask soldiers questions that every American should know. General Omar Bradley was briefly detained after he "incorrectly" identified Springfield as the capital of Illinois. The MP thought it was Chicago.

Reference:(https://en.wikipedia.org/wiki/Battle_of_the_Bulge#Operation_Greif_and_Operation_W.C3.A4hrung)

89.

Dinosaurs lived on Earth for 150 million years, while we have only been around for 0.1% of that time.

Reference: (https://www.newscientist.com/article/dn9936-top-10-dinosaur-myths/)

90.

Forest growth in the United States has exceeded harvest since the 1940s. The United States has more trees now than at any time in the past 100 years.

Reference: (http://www.mnn.com/earth-matters/wilderness-resources/stories/more-trees-than-there-were-100-years-ago-its-true)

91.

Harrison Ford was in conversations that used the same indigenous South American language in both Star Wars: A New Hope and Indiana Jones Kingdom of the Crystal Skull.

Reference:
(https://en.wikipedia.org/wiki/Quechuan_languages#In_popular_cult
ure)

92.

Truman Capote never wanted Audrey Hepburn to play Holly in "Breakfast at Tiffany's". His choice was Marilyn Monroe.

Reference:
(https://en.wikipedia.org/wiki/Breakfast_at_Tiffany%27s_(film))

93.

There is a protester named Juan who has been at the same location in Seattle, shouting the same statements for over 20 years.

Reference: (https://en.wikipedia.org/wiki/Juan_(street_protester))

94.

The iconic slow motion lifeguard run on Baywatch was due to the tight production budget. Producers were unable to film the entire 50 minute television slot, so running footage was slowed down to take up time.

Reference: (http://www.goodhollywood.com/details/david-hasselhoff-reveals-why-lifeguards-ran-in-slow-motion-on-baywatch)

95.

Six degrees of separation is the theory that everyone and everything is six or fewer steps away, by way of introduction, from any other person in the world. This would mean that a chain of "a friend of a friend" statements can be made to connect any two people in a maximum of six steps.

Reference:
(https://en.wikipedia.org/wiki/Six_degrees_of_separation)

96.

Ye Olde Cheshire Cheese Inn is a pub in London that dates back to the 16th Century and is still running. It was a favorite of Mark Twain and Charles Dickens.

Reference:
(https://en.wikipedia.org/wiki/Ye_Olde_Cheshire_Cheese)

97.

Coca-Cola bottled in Cleveland, Ohio, never switched to high-fructose corn syrup, they have always used natural sugar.

Reference: (https://en.wikipedia.org/wiki/Coca-Cola_formula)

98.

J.P. Morgan Chase is actually chartered out of Columbus, Ohio, due to its merger with Bank One.

Reference:(http://www.sec.gov/Archives/edgar/containers/fix027/10 62336/000119312504207055/dex991.htm)

99.

A study showed that United States public opinion on policies has minuscule, near-zero, statistically non-significant impact on the chance of a bill becoming law. Contrarily, economic elite's opinions have substantial impact and high correlation with policy change.

Reference: (http://journalistsresource.org/studies/politics/finance-lobbying/the-influence-of-elites-interest-groups-and-average-voters-on-american-politics)

100.

A pig in Australia stole 18 beers from a campsite, got drunk, and then attempted to fight a cow. This resulted in the cow chasing the pig around a car.

Reference: (http://gadling.com/2013/09/10/australian-pig-steals-beer/)

101.

Your own biological child can technically be older than you with time dilation.

Reference: (https://www.youtube.com/watch?v=n2s1-RHuljo)

102.

In Australia, political parties such as the Pirate Party, Sex Party, Recreational Fishers Party and the Bullet Train for Australia Party have had an actual impact in elections; and the "Motoring Enthusiasts Party" actually won a seat in the Senate.

Reference:
(https://en.wikipedia.org/wiki/List_of_political_parties_in_Australia
)

103.

Charles Barkley missed the first game of the 1994and 1995 NBA season after rubbing lotion in his eye at an Eric Clapton concert.

Reference: (http://www.nytimes.com/1994/11/04/sports/barkley-out-for-suns-opener.html)

104.

The director of the movie Cannibal Holocaust had to prove in court that he didn't murder some of the cast in some scenes.

Reference:
(https://en.wikipedia.org/wiki/Cannibal_Holocaust#Controversy)

105.

Henry Ford was not the one that invented the automobile. It was a man called Karl Benz from Germany.

Reference: (http://www.investopedia.com/articles/pf/12/auto-industry.asp)

106.

A drug used to prevent the rejection of transplanted kidneys also extends the life of elderly mice by 38%.

Reference: (http://hplusmagazine.com/2015/08/04/anti-aging-science-despite-progress-challenges-remain/)

107.

Korn's lead singer, Jonathan Davis, has a son named Zeppelin.

Reference: (https://www.youtube.com/watch?v=ps0Be3T1xkY)

108.

Ima Hogg was the name of a wealthy Texas philanthropist and she was known as the "First Lady of Texas".

Reference: (https://tshaonline.org/handbook/online/articles/fho16)

109.

In 2015, a group of students playing hide and seek in the Harris Fine Arts Center of Brigham Young University caused a faculty member to call the University Police. The police arrived but weren't able to find any of the students.

Reference: (http://universe.byu.edu/2015/10/05/police-beat-sept-25-oct1/)

110.

The most complex character in the Chinese language takes 57 strokes to write. It is a noodle dish.

Reference: (http://mentalfloss.com/article/50581/what-most-complex-chinese-character)

111.

Koko the gorilla is one of the few non-humans known to keep a pet. She has chosen herself several kittens, and named them herself. When Koko learned that one of her kittens had died, she signed "Bad, sad, bad" and "Frown, cry, frown, sad".

Reference:
(https://en.wikipedia.org/wiki/Koko_(gorilla)#Koko.27s_pets)

112.

Robyn Davidson undertook a 1,700-mile trek across Australia deserts alone with her 4 camels.

Reference: (http://proof.nationalgeographic.com/2014/09/19/rick-smolans-trek-with-tracks-from-australian-outback-to-silver-screen/)

113.

United States, India and Japan do naval exercise together. It is called Malabar.

Reference:
(https://en.wikipedia.org/wiki/Malabar_(Naval_Exercise))

114.

The game known as Rock-Paper-Scissors was originally developed in Ancient China.

Reference: (https://en.wikipedia.org/wiki/Sansukumi-ken)

115.

Billy Mitchell achieved the "perfect score" on Pac-Man in 1999, beating 256 levels and eating every pellet, fruit, and ghost, for the highest possible score of 3,333,360, without ever dying. He used his own elaborate strategies to beat the game, some of which the creators didn't even know.

Reference: (https://niume.com/pages/post/index.php?postID=23346)

116.

One of the most commonly used passwords is ncc1701, which is the serial number of the USS Enterprise, which is the main ship on Star Trek.

Reference: (http://www.cnet.com/news/yahoo-breach-swiped-passwords-by-the-numbers/)

117.

In 2014, Elon Musk opened Tesla Motors patents to the public in an attempt to encourage more competition.

Reference: (https://www.teslamotors.com/blog/all-our-patent-are-belong-you)

118.

In 1984, the New Zealand Prime Minister got drunk and decided to spontaneously call a general election, which he lost.

Reference:
(https://en.wikipedia.org/wiki/New_Zealand_general_election,_1984
)

119.

Nicolas Flamel, along with the story of the Philosopher's Stone, weren't created as works of fiction by J.K. Rowling, but rather from a real person and concept from history.

Reference: (https://en.wikipedia.org/wiki/Nicolas_Flamel)

120.

Not all Jenga pieces are the same size and shape.

Reference:
(https://en.wikipedia.org/wiki/Six_degrees_of_separation)

121.

The "long jump" used to be called the "broad jump". The name was changed because "broad" had sexist connotations.

Reference:
(http://etymonline.com/index.php?term=broad&allowed_in_frame=0
)

122.

Martin O'Malley is the founder, lead singer, and guitarist of a Celtic rock band based out of D.C. that has played at numerous shows around D.C., including the White House.

Reference:
(https://en.wikipedia.org/wiki/Martin_O%27Malley#O.27Malley.27s
_March)

123.

13 countries have the death penalty for atheism.

Reference: (http://www.huffingtonpost.com/2013/12/10/atheists-death-penalty-_n_4417994.html?t=0)

124.

Classic actors James Stewart and Henry Fonda enjoyed building model airplanes together.

Reference: (https://en.wikipedia.org/wiki/James_Stewart#cite_note-98)

125.

Saturn's moon, Titan, has an unexplained anomaly in its atmospheric composition that is consistent with earlier predictions about life there.

Reference:
(http://www.nasa.gov/topics/solarsystem/features/titan20100603.html)

126.

Hyenas are closer related to cats than dogs.

Reference: (http://www.animalfactsencyclopedia.com/Hyena-facts.html)

127.

Recent studies have shown that taking acetaminophen and ibuprofen together is actually more effective in treating pain than opioids.

Reference:
(http://www.nsc.org/RxDrugOverdoseDocuments/Evidence-Efficacy-Pain-Medications.pdf)

128.

Gordie Howe used to play with the number 17, but was offered the number 9 when a teammate left the team. Gordie accepted it because it gave him a better sleeping spot when traveling with the team.

Reference:
(https://en.wikipedia.org/wiki/Gordie_Howe#Detroit_Red_Wings)

129.

A duck's feathers are so waterproof that even when the duck dives underwater, its downy under layer of feathers will stay completely dry.

Reference: (http://birding.about.com/od/birdprofiles/a/15-Fun-Facts-About-Ducks.htm)

130.

1 in 3 women that exercise regularly will experience breast pain.

Reference: (http://well.blogs.nytimes.com/2013/05/01/the-problem-of-breast-pain-in-women-who-exercise/?ref=health)

131.

The Giant Tortoise did not receive a scientific name for over 300 years due to the failure of delivery of specimens to Europe for classification due to their great taste; all were eaten on the voyage back by sailors, even by Charles Darwin.

Reference: (http://qi.com/infocloud/giant-tortoises)

132.

Between World War I and World War II, there was a war between Poland and the Soviet Union, with Poland winning.

Reference:
(https://en.wikipedia.org/wiki/Polish%E2%80%93Soviet_War)

133.

As of 2014, Ashrita Furman has set 551 official Guinness Records and currently holds nearly 200 records, including the record for holding the most Guinness world records.

Reference: (https://en.wikipedia.org/wiki/Ashrita_Furman)

134.

A University of Manchester debate on feminism and censorship was canceled when the student union barred both speakers due to the university's "safe space" policy.

Reference:
(http://www.washingtontimes.com/news/2015/oct/7/milo-yiannopoulos-julie-bindel-banned-from-uk-univ/)

135.

Couples that cuddle can become addicted to one another. Symptoms of withdrawal can occur when apart as a result of the hormone oxytocin, "the cuddling drug."

Reference:
(http://en.wikibooks.org/wiki/Relationships/Hormones#Oxytocin)

136.

Rum was the main currency in colonial Australia. When Governor William Bligh tried to end the army officers' monopoly in the 1800's, his Government was overthrown in the only coup in Australian history.

Reference:(http://www2.sl.nsw.gov.au/archive/discover_collections/history_nation/terra_australis/rebellion/index.html)

137.

There was a briefly popular social movement in the early 1930s called the "Technocracy Movement." Technocrats proposed replacing politicians and businessmen with scientists and engineers who had the expertise to manage the economy.

Reference: (https://en.wikipedia.org/wiki/Technocracy_movement)

138.

Google has a room full of robotic arms learning hand-eye coordination to teach them how to interact with different environments.

Reference:
(http://www.popularmechanics.com/technology/robots/a20190/google-room-full-of-robot-arms/)

139.

There are three hotels in Japan which are still operational which opened before the birth of Charlemagne.

Reference: (https://en.wikipedia.org/wiki/List_of_oldest_companies)

140.

Paris Metro trains drive on the right rather than the left and its tunnels are narrower than main line ones in order to prevent it from being absorbed into the national railway network.

Reference:
(https://en.wikipedia.org/wiki/Paris_M%C3%A9tro#History)

141.

French braille is the original braille alphabet and the basis of all other braille systems. It was created by Louis Braille in 1837.

Reference: (https://en.wikipedia.org/wiki/French_Braille)

142.

A patent troll collected more than $100 million in license fees from 30 companies and sued 31 other companies for using the JPEG image format.

Reference: (https://en.wikipedia.org/wiki/Patent_troll#Causes)

143.

The washing machine and electricity had a profound impact on the lives of women, giving them the possibility to access the marketplace.

Reference:
(https://www.sciencedaily.com/releases/2009/03/090312150735.htm
)

144.

John Kasich sent a letter to President Nixon while he was a freshman in college requesting a meeting to discuss his concerns for America. He was granted a 5 minute meeting but got 20 instead.

Reference: (http://fortune.com/2012/03/12/ohio-governors-career-making-moment/)

145.

In 1921, workers at an ammonium nitrate factory tried clearing a clogged silo with dynamite. The resulting explosion killed 500 people and left 6,500 homeless.

Reference: (https://en.wikipedia.org/wiki/Oppau_explosion)

146.

The group Together, Thomas Bangalter of Daft Punk, and DJ Falcon, had made a song sampling Valerie by Steve Winwood, but had no intention to release the song.

Reference:
(https://en.wikipedia.org/wiki/Call_on_Me_(Eric_Prydz_song)#Background)

147.

Brussels is the capital of Europe because Belgium starts with letter B. European Union institutions were supposed to be chaired in turn by the ministers of each of the six member states. Belgium was the first by alphabetical order. They just never moved on to the other states.

Reference: (http://www.brusselstimes.com/opinion/860/why-did-brussels-become-the-capital-of-europe-because-belgium-starts-with-letter-b)

148.

In 1964, the inventor Karl Kroyer once filled a sunken ship with 27 million plastic balls to make it lighter and easy to remove. He then tried to patent the idea but failed as an examiner found the same method used by Donald Duck in a comic book in 1949, 15 years before.

Reference: (http://www.greyb.com/4-cases-examiner-found-ridiculously-awesome-prior-art/)

149.

A 75 year old woman was arrested after she took a hammer to a Comcast customer service center and smashed up the waiting room. She stated, "It had never occurred to me to take a hammer to a phone company before, but I was just so upset."

Reference: (http://www.washingtonpost.com/wp-dyn/content/article/2010/12/01/AR2010120104743.html)

150.

The Mortal Kombat soundtrack was the first platinum EDM record ever in history.

Reference: (http://www.hollywoodreporter.com/heat-vision/mortal-kombat-movie-oral-history-815287)

151.

Frozen is the highest grossing animated film ever released worldwide and grossed at $1,287,000,000.

Reference: (https://en.wikipedia.org/wiki/List_of_highest-grossing_animated_films)

152.

There is a sport in Scotland called "haggis hurling", in which the objective is to throw a haggis as far as possible from atop a platform. The haggis must still be edible after it lands.

Reference: (https://en.wikipedia.org/wiki/Haggis_hurling)

153.

It is possible for some people to sneeze with their eyes open.

Reference: (http://www.discovery.com/tv-shows/mythbusters/mythbusters-database/sneezing-eyeballs-pop-out/)

154.

People used to climb inside the carcass of a dead whale to cure their rheumatism.

Reference: (http://www.bbc.com/news/world-asia-pacific-26807485)

155.

Men with short index fingers and long ring fingers tend to be nicer toward women.

Reference: (http://www.livescience.com/49883-finger-length-in-men.html)

156.

In 1999, the African World Reparations and Reparation Truth Commission called for "the West" to pay $777 trillion to Africa within five years.

Reference: (http://news.bbc.co.uk/2/hi/africa/424984.stm)

157.

North Korea were recognized by Guinness World Records for having the largest mass gymnastics performance.

Reference: (https://en.wikipedia.org/wiki/Arirang_Festival)

158.

The system request key, SysReq, has no standard use.

Reference: (https://en.wikipedia.org/wiki/System_request)

159.

There's a syndrome affecting New Guinean males which leads to hyperactivity, clumsiness and even amnesia.

Reference: (https://en.wikipedia.org/wiki/Wild_man_syndrome)

160.

There are $100 coins that are legal U.S. tender. They weigh 1 ounce and are 99.95% platinum. This is the highest face value ever to appear on a U.S. coin.

Reference:(http://www.usmint.gov/mint_programs/american_eagles/?Action=american_eagle_platinum)

161.

Hungry men find women with higher body weights more attractive, according to a scientific study.

Reference: (http://www.ncbi.nlm.nih.gov/pubmed/16848948)

162.

If you park your car under a sycamore tree and it's all sticky in the morning it's not tree sap making it that way, it is greenfly droppings.

Reference:(http://www.hyndburnbc.gov.uk/site/scripts/faqs.php?categoryID=505&faqID=124#a124)

163.

Fasting and caloric restriction is actually very healthy for the brain.

Reference: (http://www.cosmicscientist.com/ted-talk-neuroscientist-shows-what-fasting-does-to-your-brain/)

164.

The London Stone is a landmark in London which consists of a block of limestone in a cage. The age and original purpose of the rock are unknown.

Reference: (https://en.wikipedia.org/wiki/London_Stone)

165.

In World War II, for every 50 Soviet causalities, there was only about 1 United States casualty.

Reference:
(http://www.nationalww2museum.org/learn/education/for-students/ww2-history/ww2-by-the-numbers/world-wide-deaths.html)

166.

Hindi, the official language spoken in India, is also the official language in Fiji.

Reference: (https://en.wikipedia.org/wiki/Hindi#Official_status)

167.

The trope of a detective using a magnifying glass was first used in "A Study in Scarlet", the first Sherlock Holmes book.

Reference: (https://en.wikipedia.org/wiki/A_Study_in_Scarlet)

168.

The band Guns'n'Roses is banned in China because of the album "Chinese Democracy".

Reference:
(https://en.wikipedia.org/wiki/Censorship_in_China#Music)

169.

Male giraffe's head-butt female giraffes in the bladder until they urinate. The male giraffe will then taste the urine to see if he can mate with her.

Reference: (http://iloveuselessknowledge.com/2015/02/03/male-giraffes-headbutt-female-giraffes-in-the-bladder-until-she-urinates-the-male-giraffe-will-then/)

170.

According to a recent study, men who posted lots of selfies, but didn't really spend time editing them, showed signs of above average psychopathy.

Reference: (http://gizmodo.com/men-who-post-selfies-online-show-signs-of-psychopathy-1678809922)

171.

After the U.S. beat Japan in the women's world cup final, Pearl Harbor became one of the top trends among Twitter users in the U.S., attracting thousands of tweets.

Reference: (http://www.bbc.com/news/world-asia-33405094)

172.

A Hungarian man was shot in the frontal lobe during World War I, making it impossible for him to fall asleep. He continued to live a full, sleepless life.

Reference: (https://trove.nla.gov.au/newspaper/article/31059591)

173.

When you sleep, you lose a measurable amount of weight in carbon atoms.

Reference:
(http://www.npr.org/sections/krulwich/2013/06/19/193556929/every
-night-you-lose-more-than-a-pound-while-youre-asleep-for-the-
oddest-reason)

174.

A 103 year old cracker from the Titanic was sold to a Greek collector for approximately $23,000 dollars at a British auction and is now known as the "World's Most Valuable Biscuit."

Reference: (http://mashable.com/2015/10/27/titanic-cracker-sold-
for-23000/#fxRB.FBGKiqg)

175.

The producers for Willy Wonka and the Chocolate Factory had a hard time finding enough little people for the role of Oompa Loompas because the Nazis killed so many during World War II.

Reference: (http://moviepilot.com/posts/3536357)

176.

The reason we don't see mosquitos in the winter is because they enter a stage of hibernation since they are cold blooded.

Reference: (http://insectcop.net/where-do-mosquitoes-go-in-the-
winter/)

177.

There are 17 different types of ice.

Reference: (https://en.wikipedia.org/wiki/Ice)

178.

During the "Happy Land Fire", 87 people were killed at a social club in the Bronx, New York, by an arsonist.

Reference: (https://en.wikipedia.org/wiki/Happy_Land_fire)

179.

Ricky Jackson spent 39 years in prison for a murder that he didn't commit.

Reference: (http://www.nbcnews.com/news/us-news/ohio-man-ricky-jackson-exonerated-after-39-years-prison-sues-n361531)

180.

Charlotte Woodward, a signatory at the landmark Seneca Falls Women's Rights Convention in 1848, lived long enough to be able to vote for president in 1920.

Reference: (http://www.nps.gov/wori/learn/historyculture/charlotte-woodward.htm)

181.

It took all of human history, up to 1804, for the world's population to reach 1 billion. The next billion came only 123 years later, in 1927.

Reference: (http://www.pbs.org/newshour/bb/world-july-dec11-population1_10-27/)

182.

Hunting for elephant ivory in Africa and Asia has led to elephants being born with shorter tusks or no tusks at all.

Reference:
(https://en.wikipedia.org/wiki/Elephant?oldformat=true#Teeth)

183.

Bluetooth was named after the 10th century, 2nd King of Denmark.

Reference: (http://www.pcworld.com/article/2061288/so-thats-why-its-called-bluetooth-and-other-surprising-tech-name-origins.html)

184.

The music that plays on the GameCube's startup screen is the startup music from the Famicom Disk System but played at one sixteenth of its original speed.

Reference: (http://www.eeggs.com/items/59536.html)

185.

The SR-71 did much more than just take pictures. It could aim its radar 45 degrees to the side, map the terrain like side scan sonar, intercept enemy communication and radar signals, and record its entire flight path with infrared cameras so it could prove to countries that it didn't violate their airspace.

Reference: (http://en.wikipedia.org/wiki/Lockheed_SR-71_Blackbird#Engines)

186.

In December, 1979, a man was killed by a flying lawnmower at a Jets game.

Reference: (http://www.sportstalkflorida.com/fan-died-drone-jets-game)

187.

The famous Bloop sound, once thought to come from an unknown marine animal, was recently attributed by NOAA to icebergs cracking.

Reference: (http://www.pmel.noaa.gov/acoustics/sounds/bloop.html)

188.

Johnny Cash originally wore black because it was the only matching color among his band members' clothes.

Reference: (https://en.wikipedia.org/wiki/Johnny_cash#Early_life)

189.

Jennifer Jackson was the first woman of color to be the centerfold in Playboy Magazine, which was published in 1965.

Reference: (https://en.wikipedia.org/wiki/Jennifer_Jackson_(model))

190.

Nazi war criminal, Friedrich Jackeln's, killing style was known as "sardine packing" and was so cruel that it horrified even some of the experienced Einsatzgruppen killers.

Reference: (https://en.wikipedia.org/wiki/Friedrich_Jeckeln)

191.

Being out of mobile phone contact is an actual phobia, called nomophobia.

Reference: (https://en.wikipedia.org/wiki/Nomophobia)

192.

Serial killer Gary Heidnik made money by investing in Playboy.

Reference: (http://murderpedia.org/male.H/h1/heidnik-gary.htm)

193.

Brazilian capital city of Brasilia is laid out to resemble an airplane.

Reference: (http://www.aboutbrasilia.com/maps/brasilia-map.php)

194.

The Irish Potato Famine is considered by many to be a genocide. British troops forcefully exported Irish livestock and crops, leaving only the blighted potato.

Reference:
(https://en.wikipedia.org/wiki/Great_Famine_(Ireland)#Genocide_qu estion)

195.

In 1954, a fifteen year old told his parents he was going to school, but then rode his bike 700 miles in a week from D.C. to Atlanta because he was "homesick for Dixie and his grandmother's fried chicken."

Reference:(http://news.google.com/newspapers?id=X0FTAAAAIB AJ&sjid=RIUDAAAAIBAJ&pg=6946%2C803725)

196.

There is a whole section of Virginia detached from the mainland and is part of the Maryland-Delaware peninsula.

Reference: (http://www.virginia.org/regions/easternshore/)

197.

There was an United States court case called "United States v. Article Consisting of 50,000 Cardboard Boxes More or Less, Each Containing One Pair of Clacker Balls".

Reference:(https://en.wikipedia.org/wiki/United_States_v._Article_Consisting_of_50,000_Cardboard_Boxes_More_or_Less,_Each_Containing_One_Pair_of_Clacker_Balls)

198.

Cannabis has been linked to schizophrenia but only for people with the COMT gene type.

Reference:
(http://www.ncbi.nlm.nih.gov/pmc/articles/PMC4033190/)

199.

"Second" as a measurement of time is called that because it's the second division of the hour after the minute.

Reference:
(http://www.etymonline.com/index.php?allowed_in_frame=0&search=Second+)

200.

Paul McCartney, a fan of Weird Al Yankovic, refused Yankovic the permission to record a parody of Wings' "Live and Let Die," titled "Chicken Pot Pie", because McCartney didn't want to condone eating meat.

Reference: (http://www.axs.com/news/when-paul-mccartney-turned-down-weird-al-album-to-debut-at-1-15046)

201.

In 2002, New York City considered helping the homeless by housing them on cruise ships.

Reference: (http://articles.latimes.com/2002/nov/21/nation/na-cruise21)

202.

Octopi are the only conscious invertebrates and have cognitive thinking abilities, individual emotions and personalities, and even form relationships with humans.

Reference: (https://orionmagazine.org/article/deep-intellect/)

203.

Nine years before Pixar released their famous animation, Luxo Jr, about a lamp, amateur filmmaker Peter Ryde made a similar stop-motion animation about three Anglepoise lamps.

Reference: (https://www.anglepoise.com/blog/2014/11/lights-camera-action)

204.

There's so much vitamin A in a polar bear's liver that it can make you severely sick if you consumed it.

Reference: (https://en.wikipedia.org/wiki/Hypervitaminosis_A#History)

205.

Japanese High School kids inadvertently gave each other pink eye as a sexual fetish by licking each other's eyeballs.

Reference: (http://tokyodesu.com/2013/06/12/school-kids-licking-each-others-eyeballs-spreading-pink-eye/)

206.

London was once supposed to have been rebuilt into an ordered grid system after the Great Fire. It never quite happened, but was the basis of the grid layout of most American cities.

Reference: (http://www.bbc.co.uk/news/magazine-35418272)

207.

Scientist have bred glow in the dark rabbits, as part of an effort to improve treatments for life-threatening illnesses.

Reference: (https://www.theguardian.com/world/2013/aug/13/glow-in-dark-rabbits-scientists)

208.

In Boston, a wife and her unborn child were robbed and killed. The surviving husband gave the vague description of the assailant as "a black man with a husky voice" throwing the city into a police state of racial unrest. It later emerged the white husband killed them for the insurance money.

Reference:
(https://en.wikipedia.org/wiki/Charles_Stuart_(murderer))

209.

Once the sea squirt becomes stationary, it eats its own brain.

Reference:
(https://www.psychologytoday.com/blog/choke/201207/how-humans-learn-lessons-the-sea-squirt)

210.

Louis Armstrong asked Richard Nixon to carry his bags through customs for him because he "was an old man". The bags actually had marijuana in them.

Reference: (http://www.veryimportantpotheads.com/armstrong.htm)

211.

Until very recently, the clitoris was severely overlooked by anatomists due to most of the studies being conducted by males.

Reference: (http://www.iflscience.com/health-and-medicine/why-clitoris-doesn-t-get-attention-it-deserves-and-why-matters)

212.

There is a rattlesnake species that has no rattle.

Reference: (https://en.wikipedia.org/wiki/Crotalus_catalinensis)

213.

The "Yadda Yadda Yadda" woman on Seinfeld is the same actress who plays Laurie Bream on Silicon Valley.

Reference: (https://en.wikipedia.org/wiki/Suzanne_Cryer)

214.

The United States Government has enacted a law titled the "Animal Crush Video Prohibition Act of 2010" in response to the animal crushing fetishists.

Reference: (https://www.gpo.gov/fdsys/pkg/STATUTE-124/pdf/STATUTE-124-Pg3177.pdf)

215.

There is a muffin shop in San Francisco, called Double or Muffin, that will double your order for free if you flip a coin and it lands on heads.

Reference: (http://doubleormuffin.com/about-us/)

216.

The translation of the word "England" from Chinese is "country of heroes".

Reference: (http://blog.mandarinportal.com/country-names-in-chinese/)

217.

Kayne West's last 7 album releases have gone to number 1 on the U.S. billboard chart.

Reference:
(https://en.wikipedia.org/wiki/Kanye_West#Discography)

218.

In 2013, PayPal accidentally credited $92 quadrillion to a Pennsylvania man.

Reference: (http://edition.cnn.com/2013/07/17/tech/paypal-error/)

219.

St. Patrick was actually British. He was captured and forced to be a slave by Irish pirates at the age of sixteen and then later escaped and fled back home. He later returned to Ireland as a Christian missionary.

Reference:(https://en.wikipedia.org/w/index.php?title=Saint_Patrick&mobileaction=toggle_view_desktop#Life)

220.

Ren Xiaofeng, a manager of The Agricultural Bank of China, stole $26,000 from the bank with the intention of buying lottery tickets, winning, and repaying the initial theft. Against the odds, it worked so he tried again with $6.7 million. He lost all of it but $95,000 and was sentenced to death.

Reference: (http://news.bbc.co.uk/2/hi/asia-pacific/6938819.stm)

221.

There is a 280-mile seawall that runs along much of Guyana's, South America, coastline to protect settlements in the coastal areas of Guyana, most of which are below sea level at high tide. An estimated 90% of population in Guyana lives below sea level.

Reference: (https://en.wikipedia.org/wiki/Sea_Wall,_Guyana)

222.

Bacteria which has evolved to be able to survive in the highly toxic Berkeley Pit superfund site produces a chemical compound not found anywhere else with anticancer potential.

Reference: (https://en.wikipedia.org/wiki/Berkeley_Pit)

223.

Zimmerit is a putty-like coating containing sawdust which some German tanks in World War II were covered with in order to prevent magnetic mines from sticking to them.

Reference: (https://en.wikipedia.org/wiki/Zimmerit)

224.

An estimated 10% to 20% of the entire population of Mauritania is enslaved. It only became a crime in 2007.

Reference:(http://edition.cnn.com/interactive/2012/03/world/mauritania.slaverys.last.stronghold/)

225.

Valentina Vassilyeva was a Russian peasant who gave birth to 69 children. None of the children were born by themselves, as she gave birth 27 times; having 16 pairs of twins, 7 sets of triples, and 4 sets of quadruplets. Fedor, her husband, later had an additional 18 children with his second wife.

Reference: (https://en.wikipedia.org/wiki/Feodor_Vassilyev)

226.

Fox Tossing was once a popular European competitive blood sport.

Reference: (https://en.wikipedia.org/wiki/Fox_tossing)

227.

There was an olive tree in Athens estimated to be about 2,400 years old and that was alleged to be a remnant of the grove in which Plato's Academy was located. It was uprooted by a bus in 1975 and its trunk is now in a local university.

Reference:
(https://en.wikipedia.org/wiki/Olive#Oldest_known_olive_trees)

228.

Japan has one of the highest incidence of stomach cancer in the world partly due to high consumption of salt, pickled and smoked food and prevalence of H. Pylori bacteria.

Reference: (http://www.livestrong.com/article/361804-japanese-diet-stomach-cancer/)

229.

Food tastes different on an airplane because of engine noise.

Reference: (http://news.health.com/2015/05/20/why-does-airplane-food-taste-bad-science-has-the-answer/)

230.

The United Kingdom government has created guidelines for how pedestrians should walk.

Reference: (https://www.gov.uk/rules-pedestrians-1-to-35/general-guidance-1-to-6)

231.

Abraham Lincoln suspended Habeas Corpus, which was an integral part of civil rights.

Reference:
(https://en.wikipedia.org/wiki/Habeas_Corpus_Suspension_Act_186
3)

232.

Vassilis Paleokostas is a man who successfully escaped prison twice via hijacked helicopter who to this day remains a fugitive.

Reference: (https://en.wikipedia.org/wiki/Vassilis_Palaiokostas)

233.

Vigdís Finnbogadóttir was the world's first female president in Iceland in 1980.

Reference:
(https://en.wikipedia.org/wiki/Vigd%C3%ADs_Finnbogad%C3%B3
ttir)

234.

The audio phenomenon called Skyquakes are unexplained booms heard in parts around the world that are similar to the breaking of the sound barrier. Several explanations have been suggested, ranging from collapsing air pockets underwater or meteors entering the atmosphere.

Reference: (http://mentalfloss.com/uk/weather/36630/what-is-a-skyquake?uk)

235.

Nude House is a computer software company in Buckinghamshire, UK, that is seeking web developers. One of their rules, however, is that no clothes are allowed in the office.

Reference: (http://www.nude-house.com/)

236.

Numerous companies and regiments adopted North African clothing on both sides of the American Civil War.

Reference: (https://en.wikipedia.org/wiki/Zouave)

237.

Steve Irwin has a snail named after him, called the Crikey steveirwini.

Reference: (https://en.wikipedia.org/wiki/Crikey_steveirwini)

238.

The perpetrator of the 2011 Norway attacks, in which he murdered 77 people, was admitted to the University of Oslo as an undergraduate in Political Science in 2015. In 2013, he was rejected because "his qualifications were lacking."

Reference:
(https://en.wikipedia.org/wiki/Anders_Behring_Breivik#Prison_life)

239.

In 1970, a group of hikers outside of Bergen, Norway, suddenly came upon the charred, naked, fingerprint-less corpse of a woman in the middle of the Isdalen Valley. The woman was nicknamed the Isdal Woman and her story remains one of Norway's deepest mysteries.

Reference: (https://en.wikipedia.org/wiki/Isdal_Woman)

240.

A notion examined by the United States military found that putting psychopaths, known as "natural born killers", at key locations during combat acts as force multipliers.

Reference:
(http://webcache.googleusercontent.com/search?q=cache:Krg-

OTvG6s0J:https://notes.utk.edu/bio/greenberg.nsf/a80806fbebea8dd
285257015006e1943/09613ff986b2a86885257599001505c1%3FOp
enDocument+&cd=1&hl=en&ct=clnk&gl=us)

241.

People overestimate food portion size on plates with wider and colored rims.

Reference:
(http://www.ncbi.nlm.nih.gov/pmc/articles/PMC3947396/)

242.

Avocados are berries.

Reference: (https://en.wikipedia.org/wiki/Avocado)

243.

In 1988, British politician Edwina Currie was forced to resign after incorrectly stating that British eggs were tainted with salmonella. A few months later, a government report found she was actually correct, but it was covered up until 2001.

Reference:
(https://en.wikipedia.org/wiki/Edwina_Currie#Salmonella_in_eggs_
controversy)

244.

With over 1600 volcanoes, Venus has more volcanoes than any other planet in the solar system.

Reference:
(http://volcano.oregonstate.edu/oldroot/volcanoes/planet_volcano/ve
nus/intro.html)

245.

Polish doctor, Eugene Lazowski, saved 8,000 Jews during the Holocaust by injecting dead typhus cells into them, allowing them to test positive for typhus despite being healthy. Germans were afraid of the highly contagious disease and refused to deport them to concentration camps.

Reference: (http://en.wikipedia.org/wiki/Eugene_Lazowski)

246.

The Florence Nightingale effect is a situation where a caregiver develops romantic and, or sexual feelings for his or her patient, even if very little communication or contact takes place outside of basic care.

Reference:
(https://en.wikipedia.org/wiki/Florence_Nightingale_effect)

247.

The Florence Nightingale effect is a situation where a caregiver develops romantic and, or sexual feelings for his or her patient, even if very little communication or contact takes place outside of basic care.

Reference:
(https://en.wikipedia.org/wiki/Florence_Nightingale_effect)

248.

"Wannabe" by Spice Girls was deemed as the U.K.'s catchiest song after a study found it only takes 2.29 seconds for listeners to recognize it.

Reference: (http://www.ibtimes.com/spice-girls-science-wannabe-makes-history-catchiest-pop-song-hooked-music-project-1717410)

249.

The German name for "Jello" translates into "food of the Gods."

Reference: (https://en.wikipedia.org/wiki/G%C3%B6tterspeise)

250.

Leather made in Bugatti Veyron's are sourced from separately raised cows in the mountains of Austria, because the cows are in an environment free of barbed wire and mosquitoes, allowing for almost flawless hide.

Reference: (https://www.youtube.com/watch?v=TwTnVI-sD04&feature=youtu.be&t=660)

251.

Some Norwegians refer to "turning it off and on again" as pushing the "Swedish button".

Reference: (https://www.nrk.no/kultur/--svenskeknappen_-1.2132725)

252.

People that can lucid dream can intentionally manipulate and direct any element of the dream experience to his or her personal desires.

Reference: (http://www.lucidipedia.com/lucid-dreaming-research/)

253.

In the U.S. and Canada, the term "gaylord" is sometimes used for triplewall corrugated pallet boxes.

Reference: (https://en.wikipedia.org/wiki/Bulk_box)

254.

The Mars Climate Orbiter Mission failed as the result of one team programming the landing based on the English system of measurement while other teams programmed it expecting the metric system to be used.

Reference: (https://en.wikipedia.org/wiki/Mars_Climate_Orbiter)

255.

NASA found "portals" between the Sun and the Earth's Magnetic fields.

Reference:
(http://www.nasa.gov/mission_pages/sunearth/news/mag-portals.html)

256.

At Facebook, if an employee's keyboard breaks, they can get a new one from a vending machine instead of waiting for IT to replace it.

Reference: (http://fortune.com/2011/07/06/facebooks-vending-machines-a-coke-or-a-keyboard/)

257.

Humans can learn self-defense through being tickled.

Reference: (http://www.popsci.com/science/article/2010-12/fyi-what-evolutionary-purpose-tickling)

258.

The word "thug" comes from Thuggees, who were professional robbers and murderers that terrorized India for 600 years. They were eventually destroyed by the British.

Reference: (https://en.wikipedia.org/wiki/Thuggee)

259.

The actor who played Spartacus in the original movie in 1960, Kirk Douglas, is still alive at the age of 99.

Reference: (https://en.wikipedia.org/wiki/Kirk_Douglas)

260.

Indian scientists can determine your blood cholesterol level from a photograph of your hand.

Reference:
(http://www.sciencedaily.com/releases/2012/08/120817135536.htm)

261.

Inhabitants of North Sentinel Island have been there for about 60,000 years. They remain completely untouched by modern civilization and kill outsiders who get too close.

Reference: (http://mentalfloss.com/article/23973/stone-age-people-north-sentinel-island)

262.

As early as 1956, there were suggestions in the scientific literature that trans-fats could be a cause of the large increase in coronary artery disease.

Reference: (https://en.wikipedia.org/wiki/Trans_fat#History)

263.

A small portion of people may have an allergic reaction to marijuana with symptoms including "hay fever," asthma, and even anaphylaxis.

Reference: (http://acaai.org/news/marijuana-allergen-you-never-knew-existed)

264.

Bats don't flap their entire forelimbs, as birds do, but instead flap their spread out digits.

Reference: (https://en.wikipedia.org/wiki/Digit_(anatomy))

265.

The Egyptian goddess Seshat, credited with the invention of writing, astronomy, architecture and mathematics, is portrayed in hieroglyphics with a cannabis leaf above her head.

Reference: (http://en.wikipedia.org/wiki/Seshat)

266.

All the names of Saiyans in the popular animated franchise, Dragon Ball Z, are vegetable puns.

Reference:
(http://dragonball.wikia.com/wiki/Origins_of_character_names)

267.

The Chinese Government attempted to cover-up the Tianjin explosion's aftermath. The explosion in the middle of the city killed more than 170 people, was the equivalent of 450 tons of TNT, and had drastic effects on the environment.

Reference:
(http://www.washingtontimes.com/news/2015/aug/20/inside-china-tianjin-explosions-cover-up-exposes-b/)

268.

Joseph Stalin had his secret police set up a department whose aim was to obtain foreign leader's feces and analyze them in an attempt to construct psychological portraits.

Reference: (http://www.bbc.co.uk/news/world-asia-35427926)

269.

Native American warrior Crazy Horse grew to hate white people after witnessing his tribe being attacked by U.S. troops. They had come because his tribe had slaughtered a cow that accidentally wandered into their village.

Reference: (https://en.wikipedia.org/wiki/Crazy_Horse#Visions)

270.

The entire country of Liechtenstein can be rented for $70,000 a day.

Reference: (http://blog.airbnb.com/rent-anything-from-a-couchto-a-country/)

271.

"Vacuum Decay" is a terrifying universe-death scenario in which quantum fluctuations could cause our metastable, "false vacuum" world to revert to a state of "true vacuum" in a bubble of oblivion that expands outwards at the speed of light. It could happen at any time for no reason.

Reference: (https://cosmosmagazine.com/physical-sciences/vacuum-decay-ultimate-catastrophe)

272.

The smell of freshly cut grass is actually the grass sending out a SOS signal and trying to heal itself from the trauma it receives when it is cut.

Reference: (http://mentalfloss.com/article/30573/what-causes-fresh-cut-grass-smell?utm_source=Facebook&utm_medium=Partner&utm_campaign=DYK)

273.

Rather than use CGI, Tim Burton had 40 squirrels trained to crack nuts for Charlie and The Chocolate Factory.

Reference:
(http://news.bbc.co.uk/2/hi/uk_news/magazine/4702653.stm)

274.

A Tamil-American scientist Dr. Shiva Ayyadurai created and copyrighted a software called "EMAIL" in 1982. He claims that he is the true inventor of e-mail and that his undergraduate professor, Noam Chomsky, supports his claims.

Reference:(https://en.wikipedia.org/wiki/Shiva_Ayyadurai#Development_of_software_named_.22EMAIL.22_and_controversy_about_its_relation_to_email)

275.

Humanity First is an international charitable trust that cites efficiencies resulting in over 93% of funds going straight to projects, and the actual aid value delivered is often 50 times greater than the value of donations received.

Reference: (https://en.wikipedia.org/wiki/Humanity_First)

276.

The original TRON movie wasn't nominated for a special-effects Oscar because the Motion Picture Academy thought they "cheated by using computers."

Reference: (http://entertainment.time.com/2012/02/17/top-10-memorable-movie-motorcycles/slide/tron/)

277.

Kenneth Anderson, like Jim Corbett, liberated pre-independence India of several man eating tigers and leopards.

Reference:
(https://en.wikipedia.org/wiki/Kenneth_Anderson_(writer))

278.

Some astronauts need a new prescription for their glasses after returning to Earth. That is, if they've spent at least 6 months or more in space.

Reference: (http://www.geteyesmart.org/eyesmart/eye-health-news/space-flight-and-vision.cfm)

279.

A French mathematician, the day before his duel, published all his work because he didn't think that he would survive. The next day, he died at the age of 20 from a bullet to his gut.

Reference: (http://www.storyofmathematics.com/19th_galois.html)

280.

A man who spent 6 months in jail after being falsely accused of murder was set free when his attorney established his alibi by finding him in outtake footage from, "Curb Your Enthusiasm," which was shooting at a Dodgers game.

Reference: (http://www.cbsnews.com/news/hbo-video-curbs-police-enthusiasm/)

281.

There is a town in Pennsylvania called Centralia, where a coal mine started burning in 1962 and has been burning ever since.

Reference: (http://www.centraliapa.org/)

282.

Between 2012 and 2014, France had a 75% super tax on earnings above €1 million euros.

Reference:
(https://www.theguardian.com/world/2014/dec/31/france-drops-75percent-supertax)

283.

There's an unfinished Orson Welles movie which Peter Bogdanovich has been trying to finish for 30 years.

Reference:
(https://en.wikipedia.org/wiki/The_Other_Side_of_the_Wind)

284.

There was a relatively popular band in the 1980s and 1990s called Holy Soldier, which played Christian Glam Metal.

Reference: (https://en.wikipedia.org/wiki/Holy_Soldier)

285.

When Leonardo DiCaprio was acting in "Titanic", he carried his pet lizard around with him at the movie set.

Reference: (http://news.moviefone.com/2013/05/10/18-things-you-didnt-know-about-leonardo-dicaprio/)

286.

There are 54 tanks of liquid nitrogen unprotected on the streets of New York. They are used to cool underground cables and have to be replaced every 3 days. Despite being knocked over by cars, no tanks have exploded and there have been no major leaks.

Reference: (http://www.popsci.com/those-nitrogen-canisters-nyc-streets-are-keeping-your-internet-cables-cool)

287.

Fish scales are used in lipstick to make it shimmer and reflect light.

Reference: (http://www.huffingtonpost.com/entry/fish-scales-lipstick_n_7126716.html?section=india)

288.

One of the ROV's in "Titanic" was named Snoop Dog.

Reference:
(http://jamescameronstitanic.wikia.com/wiki/DUNCAN_and_Snoop
_Dog.)

289.

In the 2011 Tohoku Earthquake, residents of Sendai received 10 to 30 second warnings while Tokyo received a 60 second warning from Japan's Earthquake Early Warning system before the major seismic waves hit.

Reference: (http://spectrum.ieee.org/tech-talk/computing/networks/japans-earthquake-earlywarning-system-worked)

290.

Nigerian 419 scammers convinced Banco Noroeste executives to deposit $242 million into their Cayman bank accounts.

Reference: (http://www.assetrecovery.org/kc/node/b7b13256-28f7-11de-900c-81c63910293a.0;jsessionid=318C26C77EE43FD7D9063A2DB5C9069B)

291.

Scientific studies show that genetics plays little if any role in the development of antisocial personality disorder.

Reference:
(http://www.godandscience.org/apologetics/sociopathy_and_god.html)

292.

Earwax has been used by anthropologists to track human migratory patterns.

Reference: (https://en.wikipedia.org/wiki/Earwax)

293.

The most isolated human being ever was Al Worden, the command module pilot of Apollo 15, who in lunar orbit was at a maximum distance of 2,235 miles from his fellow astronauts on the surface. While on the other side of the moon, no communication with Earth or his comrades was possible.

Reference:
(https://en.wikipedia.org/wiki/Alfred_Worden#NASA_career)

294.

A Pakistani squash player, Jahangir Khan, won 555 matches consecutively. This is the longest winning streak by any athlete in top-level professional sports as recorded by the Guinness World Records.

Reference: (https://en.wikipedia.org/wiki/Jahangir_Khan)

295.

An 11 year old boy was sentenced to life in an adult prison.

Reference: (http://www.huffingtonpost.com/pat-nolan/11-year-olds-dont-belong_b_252541.html)

296.

Gevork Vartanian, a Soviet Armenian spy operating in Iran, led a team in 1943 that helped foil a Nazi plot to assassinate Churchill, Roosevelt and Stalin, who were meeting at Tehran Conference.

Reference: (https://en.wikipedia.org/wiki/Operation_Long_Jump)

297.

British SAS assisted in the siege of the Waco Texas compound in 1993.

Reference: (http://sasspecialairservice.com/campaigns/chronology-major-sas-operations/)

298.

Self-control in early childhood can be used to accurately predict health, wealth and criminal tendencies of people as adults.

Reference: (http://www.pnas.org/content/108/7/2693.full)

299.

The Spiny Anteater shows no interest in mating while in captivity and, therefore, no one has even seen one ejaculate. There have been attempts, trying to force them to ejaculate through the use of electrically stimulated ejaculation, but it has only results in its penis swelling.

Reference: (https://en.wikipedia.org/wiki/Echidna#Reproduction)

300.

A man spent $600 a day on the Florida Lotto, racking up to $600,000 in debt before hitting the jackpot.

Reference: (https://www.youtube.com/watch?v=pBeAEa7qAbs)

301.

Madison Bumgarner dated a girl named Madison Bumgarner.

Reference:
(https://en.wikipedia.org/wiki/Madison_Bumgarner#Personal_life)

302.

Dana Bash from CNN was previously married to fellow anchor John King, and they still work together.

Reference: (https://en.wikipedia.org/wiki/Dana_Bash)

303.

With the exception of Lyndon Johnson, every president's life since John F. Kennedy has been threatened with assassination.

Reference:(https://en.wikipedia.org/wiki/List_of_United_States_presidential_assassination_attempts_and_plots)

304.

Spandau Ballet is the name given to the spasmodic "dance" that soldiers did in World War II after being shot by the German MG-42 machine gun.

Reference: (http://www.namepistol.com/bands/definitive-27-worst-band-names-ever-20-11.html)

305.

The Chinese Han Empire was aware of the Roman Empire and they sent envoys to each other.

Reference: (https://en.wikipedia.org/wiki/Sino-Roman_relations)

306.

Steven Spielberg refused to accept any payment for his work on "Schindler's List", considering any fee he might receive to be "blood money."

Reference: (http://www.moviefone.com/2013/12/15/schindlers-list-facts/)

307.

There is an asteroid named after ASCII.

Reference: (https://en.wikipedia.org/wiki/3568_ASCII)

308.

The geographical center of the Earth is Çorum, Turkey, according to a study done in 2003.

Reference:
(https://en.wikipedia.org/wiki/Geographical_centre_of_Earth#History_of_geo-centroid_calculation)

309.

Chinese mathematician Yitang Shang couldn't get an academic job upon graduating, having to work as an accountant and a delivery worker for a New York City restaurant. He later went on to solve a math problem that had been unsolved for 150 years and won a MacArthur Genius Grant.

Reference: (https://en.wikipedia.org/wiki/Yitang_Zhang)

310.

In the Mountain Meadows Massacre of 1857, a gang of Mormons ganged up to attack a wagon train of families in Southern Utah. The aggressors pretended to be Native Americans; when they feared being discovered by the victims, they murdered about 120 people in order to avoid witnesses.

Reference:
(https://en.wikipedia.org/wiki/Mountain_Meadows_massacre)

311.

One theory says the reason for the pleasure we feel when cracking our joints repetitively is that during the process, our body releases endogenous opiates and endorphins, which are "addictive" in nature.

Reference: (http://www.causeof.org/endorphins.htm)

312.

In 1994, presidents of two countries were assassinated in one hit; they were the Rwandan and Burundian presidents.

Reference: (https://en.wikipedia.org/wiki/Assassination_of_Juv%C3%A9nal_Habyarimana_and_Cyprien_Ntaryamira)

313.

The movie "Die Hard with a Vengeance" has the title in Denmark as "Die Hard: Mega Hard".

Reference: (https://da.wikipedia.org/wiki/Die_Hard:_Mega_Hard)

314.

Here Comes the Mummies is a funk band that is rumored to have several Grammy winners among the members. They perform while wearing full mummy costumes so they can keep their identities "under wraps."

Reference:
(https://en.wikipedia.org/wiki/Here_Come_the_Mummies)

315.

The more expensive the car, the more likely the driver is to cut off pedestrians and other cars on the road.

Reference: (http://articles.latimes.com/2012/feb/27/science/la-sci-0228-greed-20120228)

316.

When German engineers were developing the MP3 file format, they used Suzanne Vega's Capella song "Tom's Diner" to test their creation, checking for loss of fidelity. She is now unofficially known as the "Mother of The MP3".

Reference:
(https://en.wikipedia.org/wiki/Tom%27s_Diner#The_.22Mother_of_the_MP3.22)

317.

In December 2015, it was discovered that a database containing the voter registrations of 191 million Americans had been leaked online. The database included information regarding first and last names, recent addresses and phone numbers, party affiliation, voting history and demographics.

Reference: (http://www.nytimes.com/2015/12/31/us/politics/voting-records-released-privacy-concerns.html?_r=1)

318.

The name "Ponzi Scheme" originated with Charles Ponzi, who promised 50% returns on investments in only 90 days in the 1920s.

Reference: (https://en.wikipedia.org/wiki/Charles_Ponzi)

319.

If you follow the recommendations from the brewery, it takes over two minutes to pour a pint of Guinness.

Reference: (http://learn.kegerator.com/pouring-guinness/)

320.

If a Canadian moose has their mate die, they will seclude themselves from the rest of their group and mourn for an indefinite amount of time.

Reference: (http://www.canadageese.org/faq4.html)

321.

Over 100 million people watched the finale of Roots in 1977. This was about 50% of the U.S. population at the time. It remains one of the most-viewed shows in history.

Reference: (http://www.museum.tv/eotv/roots.htm)

322.

Memories are created from scratch, therefore, in the process, it's different every time you remember it.

Reference: (http://www.radiolab.org/story/91569-memory-and-forgetting/)

323.

Brandon Lee, the main actor in the film "The Crow," was shot and killed on set by a firearm that was mishandled by the crew.

Reference:
(https://en.wikipedia.org/wiki/The_Crow_(1994_film)#Brandon_Lee
.27s_death)

324.

Ferdinand Demara, an imposter, served on a Canadian warship under a false identity. When a group of injured soldiers needed surgery, he successfully pulled it off by reading the medical handbook a few days before.

Reference:(http://content.time.com/time/specials/packages/article/0,
28804,1900621_1900618_1900605,00.html)

325.

Mathematicians have jokingly proposed a standard unit of measurement for beauty: the "millihelen". Inspired by Helen of Troy, a millihelen is defined as "the amount of beauty required to launch one ship."

Reference:
(http://en.wikipedia.org/wiki/List_of_humorous_units_of_measurem
ent#Non-conventional)

326.

There have been many scientific studies trying to figure out how many licks does it take to get to the center of a Tootsie Pop. Some even invented licking machines, with one being a rotating mechanical tongue.

Reference:
(https://en.wikipedia.org/wiki/Tootsie_Pop#Rumors_and_set_attemp
ts)

327.

French words for "male lawyer" and "avocado" are the same.

Reference: (http://www.collinsdictionary.com/dictionary/french-english/avocat)

328.

When Nickelodeon Studios at Universal shut down, half of it became the first official Blue Man Group Theater, and the other half has remained abandoned.

Reference: (https://www.youtube.com/watch?v=ItPkMIumy_o)

329.

The open end of a noose is called a "Honda."

Reference: (https://en.wikipedia.org/wiki/Noose)

330.

McDonalds' own employee health benefits page warned employees to avoid their own burgers and fries out of health concerns.

Reference: (https://www.rt.com/usa/mcdonalds-employees-fast-food-764/)

331.

Jackie Chan's birth name is Kong-sang Chan and he got the name Jackie while working as a construction worker in Canberra, Australia.

Reference: (http://www.jackiechankids.com/files/Jackie_Bio.htm)

332.

Road asphalt used to be a patented technology in the United States. It was only in 1920, after the expiry of the bestselling Bitulithic's patent, that the government began asphalt research and development and forced all other competitors from the market.

Reference:(http://www.asphaltpavement.org/index.php?option=com_content&task=view&id=21&Itemid=41)

333.

At Chicago's O'Hare Airport, a 20 year old Bill Murray made a joke to another passenger that he was carrying 2 bombs. Overheard by a ticket agent, a couple of U.S. marshals were summoned to search his luggage. They didn't find any bombs but rather $20,000 worth of pot. Murray was then arrested.

Reference:
(http://www.esquire.com/entertainment/movies/a37799/the-time-bill-murray-got-busted-for-pot/)

334.

Lojban is a constructed language based on formal logic and was designed to be neutral between cultures allowing you to communicate more concisely, such as being gender neutral, no tenses, and the ability to speak in emoticons.

Reference: (https://en.wikipedia.org/wiki/Lojban)

335.

The Nobel Peace Prize is awarded annually according to guidelines laid down in Alfred Nobel's will.

Reference:
(http://nobelpeaceprize.org/en_GB/about_peaceprize/history/)

336.

Ancient stone slabs in Japan had the following message: "High dwellings are the peace and harmony of our descendants. Remember the calamity of the great tsunamis. Do not build any homes below this point."

Reference: (http://www.denverpost.com/2011/04/06/stone-slabs-offer-centuries-old-tsunami-warnings-in-japan/)

337.

The FCC relocated FM radio to its current range in 1945 to undermine the finances of the inventor of FM radio, Edwin Armstrong. RCA's David Sarnoff instigated the move to protect his company's profits from superior technology.

Reference: (https://www.damninteresting.com/the-tragic-birth-of-fm-radio/#)

338.

The term "Oh the humanity!" was first popularized by the news reporter Herbert Morrison at the site of the Hindenburg Disaster.

Reference:
(https://en.wikipedia.org/wiki/Herbert_Morrison_(announcer))

339.

There is a Svalbard Global Seed Vault in Norway where the seeds of the world are kept in case of a global catastrophe.

Reference:
(https://en.wikipedia.org/wiki/Svalbard_Global_Seed_Vault)

340.

A bidet is considered a key green technology and uses significantly less water, electricity, and wood than a single roll of toilet paper.

Reference: (http://www.scientificamerican.com/article/earth-talks-bidets/)

341.

There is a "Gate Tower Building" in Osaka, Japan, with an express highway running through it.

Reference: (http://www.amusingplanet.com/2012/01/gate-tower-building-with-highway.html)

342.

The Homeowners Associations cannot adopt "Adult Swim" times because it discriminates against children.

Reference: (http://www.davis-stirling.com/MainIndex/PoolDiscrimination/tabid/1232/Default.aspx)

343.

There's been an annual Big Lebowski festival since 2002.

Reference: (https://lebowskifest.com/achiever-nation/lebowski-fest-photos/)

344.

In 1968, the Democratic National Convention selected Hubert Humphrey as the party's nominee, even though he hadn't entered a single primary.

Reference:
(https://en.wikipedia.org/wiki/1968_Democratic_National_Convention)

345.

National Airlines Flight 27 suffered an uncontained engine failure which broke a window and sucked a passenger out. His skeletal remains were found by VLA construction workers two years later.

Reference:
(http://en.wikipedia.org/wiki/National_Airlines_Flight_27)

346.

In 1990, an unemployed French physicist invaded a channel island and was tricked into giving his gun to the island's constable. He tried and failed again the following year.

Reference: (https://en.wikipedia.org/wiki/Sark#Invasion_attempt)

347.

Vibrators are illegal in Alabama.

Reference: (https://www.vice.com/read/fucking-hysterical-a-timeline-of-vintage-vibrators)

348.

The Ern Malley Hoax occurred in 1943 when, imitating the modernist poetry they despised, McAuley and Stewart submitted "bad" poems to expose the modernist magazine "Angry Penguins". Since the 1970s, however, the poems have become celebrated and are more widely read than those of their creators.

Reference: (https://en.wikipedia.org/wiki/Ern_Malley)

349.

There are no women players in the Top 100 Go players.

Reference: (http://www.axialflow.com/projects.htm)

350.

Steve Jobs "eliminated all corporate philanthropy programs" at Apple when he became CEO and declined to join Bill Gates' "Giving Pledge".

Reference:
(http://www.washingtonpost.com/business/economy/record-thin-on-steve-jobss-philanthropy/2011/10/06/gIQA3YKKRL_story.html)

351.

The "three lines" menu button is called as the "Hamburger button" due to its resemblance to a hamburger.

Reference: (https://en.wikipedia.org/wiki/Hamburger_button)

352.

Within Jamaica, there exist 11 settlements populated by descendants of Africans who escaped from slavery and established free communities. These autonomous societies maintain their traditional African celebrations and practices to this day.

Reference: (https://en.wikipedia.org/wiki/Jamaican_Maroons)

353.

The current version of the U.S. flag was designed in 1958 by 17 year old Robert Heft. He created the flag design for a high school class project. He received a B−.

Reference:
(https://en.wikipedia.org/wiki/Flag_of_the_United_States#Creation)

354.

The abbreviation "OMG" was first used in a 1917 letter to Winston Churchill.

Reference: (http://www.goratings.org/)

355.

Director, James Cameron, fell ill while in Rome during the release of Piranha II: The Spawning and had a dream about a metallic torso dragging itself from an explosion while holding kitchen knives. When Cameron returned to California, he wrote a draft to The Terminator.

Reference:
(https://en.wikipedia.org/wiki/The_Terminator?GRSEBF#Developm
ent)

356.

John Fogerty of the band Creedence Clearwater Revival tried to sue the British band the Hollies for their 1972 song "Long Cool Woman in a Black Dress" because he thought it infringed on their trademark sound used in the CCR song "Green River".

Reference:
(https://en.wikipedia.org/wiki/Long_Cool_Woman_in_a_Black_Dre
ss)

357.

The ship MV Liemba is the last remaining ship of the Imperial German Navy. She is currently a passenger and cargo ferry in Lake Tanganyika, Africa.

Reference: (https://en.wikipedia.org/wiki/MV_Liemba)

358.

One of Vincent Van Gogh's "Sunflower" paintings was destroyed on the day that the Hiroshima atomic bomb detonated, during an American bombing raid on the city Ashiya. The Japanese collector who owned the painting could not rescue it from the flames because the elaborate frame was too heavy.

Reference:
(https://www.theguardian.com/artanddesign/2013/sep/04/van-gogh-lost-sunflower-paintings)

359.

There are now about $1.2 billion dollar coin assets in the Federal Reserve vaults.

Reference: (http://www.npr.org/2011/06/28/137394348/-1-billion-that-nobody-wants)

360.

Pink Floyd played live in the BBC studio during the Apollo 11 Moon Landing.

Reference:(https://www.youtube.com/watch?v=cVHGLdZQgEw&feature=youtu.be&t=19m18s)

361.

There are tribal civilizations in Brazil that we know nothing about, other than that they exist. Not even their name, population, or general region of inhabitance.

Reference: (https://en.wikipedia.org/wiki/Uncontacted_peoples)

362.

A 2010 study found a relation between attractiveness and intelligence. More attractive individuals are more likely to have a higher IQ, and this relation was found to be slightly stronger with men than women.

Reference: (http://personal.lse.ac.uk/kanazawa/pdfs/i2011.pdf)

363.

A bear cub named Tahoe was found crying and hugging her dead mother and the rescuer, told by authorities to leave her alone, decided to save the cub instead.

Reference: (http://www.nbcnews.com/news/us-news/mystery-unbearably-cute-cub-named-tahoe-solved-n90961)

364.

Melanie Griffith lived with a lion, was attacked by a lioness and required 50 facial stitches.

Reference: (http://mashable.com/2014/10/06/yes-thats-just-the-pet-lion-in-the-swimming-pool/?utm_cid=mash-com-fb-main-link#p8ZKK_yUakq3)

365.

In 1974, a man stole a helicopter, flew it to Washington, D.C. and hovered for six minutes over the White House before descending on the south lawn. He only spent 1 year in prison and was fined $2,400 for this.

Reference: (http://nymag.com/daily/intelligencer/2014/09/weird-white-house-intruders-security-breeches.html)

366.

The Erie Canal is still in use today. With canal barges capable of hauling a short ton of cargo 514 miles on one gallon of diesel compared to trucks averaging 59 miles, the canal remains commercially practical today.

Reference: (https://en.wikipedia.org/wiki/Erie_Canal#21st_century)

367.

Grits and Polenta are made from corn.

Reference: (http://www.thekitchn.com/polenta-versus-grits-whats-the-difference-187807)

368.

There is a gravitational anomaly deep in intergalactic space called The Great Attractor. It is thousands of times more massive than our galaxy, and we're moving toward it.

Reference: (http://www.universetoday.com/113150/what-is-the-great-attractor/)

369.

A massive typhoon would have seriously hampered the planned Allied invasion of Japan if the Japanese hadn't surrendered.

Reference: (https://www.washingtonpost.com/news/capital-weather-gang/wp/2015/07/16/how-typhoons-at-the-end-of-world-war-ii-swamped-u-s-ships-and-nearly-saved-japan-from-defeat/)

370.

Lycaenidae moths chemically subdue ants to defend the moth's pupae and are able to communicate with the ants via vibrations.

Reference: (http://en.m.wikipedia.org/wiki/Lycaenidae)

371.

The Human Killing Machine is an alternate sequel of the Street Fighter series.

Reference: (https://en.wikipedia.org/wiki/Human_Killing_Machine)

372.

There is a bar in Barcelona where the beer prices change based on demand. It's called the Dow Jones Bar.

Reference: (http://dowjonesbar.com/)

373.

Animal erythrocytes have cell surface antigens that undergo polymorphism and give rise to blood types.

Reference: (https://en.wikipedia.org/wiki/Blood_type_(non-human))

374.

Although St. Patrick is famous for ridding Ireland of snakes, there was no evidence of there being snakes in Ireland in the first place.

Reference: (http://www.reptilesmagazine.com/Snakes/Information-News/Did-St-Patrick-Really-Banish-Snakes-From-Ireland/)

375.

A secretary told Steve Jobs she was late for work because her car wouldn't start. Jobs came back the same afternoon and threw her a set of keys for a brand new Jaguar saying: "Here, don't be late anymore".

Reference: (http://www.wral.com/news/local/story/10230791/)

376.

The name for the math's constant "Pi" is derived from the first letter of the Greek word "perimetros", which means circumference.

Reference: (https://en.wikipedia.org/wiki/Pi)

377.

Prisons in Uganda have only a 30% recidivism rate compared to 70% in the U.S.

Reference: (https://www.viceland.com/en_us/video/luzira-upper-prison/57210eb733a2543d47103401)

378.

Stanley Kubrick had an extensive and rich friendship with Malcom McDowell during the filming of "A Clockwork Orange". After the film was completed, Kubrick never contacted him again.

Reference:
(http://www.dailyherald.com/article/20110811/entlife/708129973/)

379.

Cassius Clay was only TKO'd once in his amateur boxing career, by a man named Kent Green in the second round in 1958. Clay was 16 years old at the time and, eventually, it would prove to be one of only two stoppage losses in the entire career of Muhammad Ali.

Reference:
(http://archives.chicagotribune.com/1979/12/16/page/276/article/the-shafting-of-alis-ghost/)

380.

Apollo 13 Astronaut, Jim Lovell, had a cameo in the movie, Apollo 13. He requested to play the captain of the ship that rescues him, because that was the same rank he held when he retired from the Navy.

Reference: (https://en.wikipedia.org/wiki/Jim_Lovell#Later_career)

381.

Tom Hiddleston originally auditioned to play Thor.

Reference: (https://www.youtube.com/watch?v=wtLLls2nbyI)

382.

Flashblood is a process in which someone injects themselves with the blood of someone else who had just injected heroin.

Reference: (https://en.wikipedia.org/wiki/Flashblood)

383.

President Cleveland said to 5-year-old Franklin D. Roosevelt, "My little man, I am making a strange wish for you. It is that you may never be president of the United States."

Reference: (http://carlanthonyonline.com/2013/01/24/the-president-who-ignored-another-presidents-advice-dont-take-this-job/)

384.

The made up word "ghoti," was pronounced the same way as "fish."

Reference: (https://www.englishclub.com/esl-articles/199909.htm)

385.

There is a humanoid robot called "Robonaut 2" that helps astronauts on the International Space Station.

Reference:
(https://www.youtube.com/watch?v=g3u48T4Vx7k&feature=youtu.be)

386.

57 people in the U.S. have been sentenced to death to later be proven innocent, since 1976.

Reference: (http://www.pnas.org/content/111/20/7230.abstract)

387.

There is only one town in Pennsylvania, and it's called Bloomsburg.

Reference:
(https://en.wikipedia.org/wiki/Bloomsburg,_Pennsylvania)

388.

The ancient Maya viewed crossed-eyes, flattened foreheads, and pointy teeth as beautiful.

Reference: (https://en.wikipedia.org/wiki/Maya_society)

389.

A Swede faced a world-record speeding fine of $1 million dollars after being caught going 170 KMH over the limit in Switzerland.

Reference: (http://www.bbc.com/news/world-europe-10960230)

390.

Some chimpanzees and monkeys have entered the Stone Age.

Reference: (http://www.bbc.co.uk/earth/story/20150818-chimps-living-in-the-stone-age)

391.

Iolani Palace in Hawaii is the only royal palace on U.S. soil.

Reference: (https://en.wikipedia.org/wiki/%CA%BBIolani_Palace)

392.

Sam Kinison, a foul-mouthed standup comic with politically incorrect humor, was a Pentecostal preacher before starting his career in comedy.

Reference: (https://en.wikipedia.org/wiki/Sam_Kinison#Early_life)

393.

The Germans massacred over 60,000 Africans before World War I, during the Herero Wars.

Reference: (https://en.wikipedia.org/wiki/Herero_Wars)

394.

When Johnny Rotten's father demanded that his son cut his long hair, Johnny had it cut short, but dyed it bright green in an act of rebellion.

Reference: (https://en.wikipedia.org/wiki/John_Lydon)

395.

During the first Moon landing, the average age of NASA controllers was 26 years old.

Reference: (http://www.pbs.org/wgbh/nova/tothemoon/kranz.html)

396.

There is a town on the Chinese and Myanmar border that is a huge gambling town and a black market wildlife trading hotspot.

Reference: (https://news.vice.com/article/the-largest-illegal-wildlife-market-in-asia-may-be-on-the-myanmar-china-border)

397.

Exercise Tiger, the training for D-Day that ended with 946 American deaths, occurred when 9 German E-boats showed up during the rehearsal and attacked.

Reference: (http://www.npr.org/2012/04/28/151590212/operation-tiger-d-days-disastrous-rehearsal)

398.

Until 1993, the choice of first names was dictated by French laws that decreed which names were acceptable.

Reference: (http://www.nytimes.com/1995/11/11/style/11iht-coco.t.html)

399.

The Roman Empire didn't exist until after Julius Caesar was assassinated. His adopted son, Augustus, returned and overthrew those who killed Caesar, then Augustus established the Empire. Augustus lived to be 75 years old, passing the Empire on to his own adopted son, Tiberius.

Reference: (https://en.wikipedia.org/wiki/Augustus)

400.

Marie Antoinette never actually said "Let them eat cake," and the quote was likely misattributed as propaganda for the French Revolution.

Reference: (https://en.wikipedia.org/wiki/Let_them_eat_cake)

401.

Despite Toyota's long list of sports cars and race heritage, the only factory Supercharged AWD car they made was the Toyota Previa, which is a minivan.

Reference: (https://en.wikipedia.org/wiki/Toyota_Previa)

402.

In 2008, a smoking ban at 18 prisons in Canada was reversed within a week after a prison riot.

Reference: (http://libcom.org/news/prisoner-riot-reverses-smoking-ban-09022008)

403.

They use the down wash from helicopters to dry cherry orchards to prevent cracking.

Reference: (http://www.environmentalbiophysics.org/sensor-data-improves-cherry-production/)

404.

Bansky was inspired by graffiti artist Robert Del Naja, who is known as "3D", who later become a founding member of the English musical group Massive Attack.

Reference: (https://en.wikipedia.org/wiki/Banksy)

405.

A lot of that weird and creepy music in horror movies is performed on one unique instrument called a waterphone.

Reference: (https://www.youtube.com/watch?v=9d1yDCWicf0)

406.

Historians found European queens have been associated with a 27% increase in wars compared to European kings.

Reference: (http://nymag.com/scienceofus/2016/01/european-queens-waged-more-wars-than-kings.html)

407.

The red and white pole outside barber shops references a time when barbers were expected to perform bloodletting and other medical procedures to heal the sick; red represented blood and white represented bandages.

Reference: (https://wikipedia.org/wiki/Barber's_pole)

408.

Shaving a dog for the summer can cause more harm than good, as their coats act as insulation.

Reference: (http://www.aspca.org/news/heat-wave-should-you-shave-your-pet)

409.

Albertville, France's electricity is powered by Beaufort cheese. Since whey is unnecessary to make Beaufort cheese, bacteria is added to the whey. This transforms the whey into biogas. This gas is then fed through an engine which heats water to 90 degrees Celsius or 194 degrees Fahrenheit to generate 2800 MWh per year of electricity.

Reference: (http://www.citylab.com/tech/2015/12/this-french-power-plant-runs-on-cheese/422034/)

410.

A common shrew's metabolism is so high that it could starve to death in mere hours.

Reference: (https://en.wikipedia.org/wiki/Common_shrew)

411.

Billions of dollars in oil are traded every year using Yahoo Messenger.

Reference: (http://news.bbc.co.uk/2/hi/business/7250554.stm)

412.

Pyrus calleryana is a deciduous tree that's common throughout North America. It blossoms in early spring and produces beautiful, five-petaled white flowers that smell like semen.

Reference: (https://theawl.com/your-street-probably-smells-like-semen-right-now-but-it-might-not-next-spring-90880b2d941c#.qhqkq125n)

413.

The creator of peanut M&Ms was allergic to peanuts.

Reference: (http://mentalfloss.com/article/68189/creator-peanut-mms-was-allergic-peanuts)

414.

The concept of toed shoes was featured on Married with Children, 8 years before minimalist shoes were invented.

Reference:
(http://marriedwithchildren.wikia.com/wiki/Episode:God's_Shoes)

415.

The first self-made millionaire woman in America was African American and she was the first freeborn person in her family.

Reference: (https://en.wikipedia.org/wiki/Madam_C._J._Walker)

416.

Nearly 1 in 5 people in South Africa are HIV positive.

Reference: (https://www.avert.org/professionals/hiv-around-world/sub-saharan-africa/south-africa)

417.

Merv Griffin originally gained fame for singing the hit 1950 song "I've got a lovely bunch of coconuts."

Reference: (https://en.wikipedia.org/wiki/Merv_Griffin#Singing)

418.

Singer Merry Clayton suffered a miscarriage that some sources attribute to her exertions during the recording of "Gimme Shelter".

Reference: (https://en.wikipedia.org/wiki/Gimme_Shelter)

419.

There is no Nobel Prize for Mathematics because Alfred Nobel didn't want one.

Reference:
(http://www.nobelprize.org/faq/questions_in_category.php?id=2)

420.

Jehovah's Witnesses teach that Satan and his demons were cast down to Earth from Heaven 100 years ago. This would mean that the event occurred in 1916.

Reference: (https://en.wikipedia.org/wiki/Jehovah%27s_Witnesses)

421.

Elijah Wood urinated in an iconic New Zealand fountain during the filming of the Lord of the Rings.

Reference: (https://en.wikipedia.org/wiki/The_Bucket_Fountain)

422.

"Just a moment" literally means you're giving yourself 90 seconds to finish or perform whatever was in question.

Reference: (https://en.wikipedia.org/wiki/Moment_(time))

423.

Norma McCorvey, Roe in Roe v. Wade, became pregnant twice after coming out as a lesbian, which she later recanted.

Reference: (https://en.wikipedia.org/wiki/Norma_McCorvey)

424.

It took mathematicians 358 years to successfully solve Fermat's Last Theorem.

Reference:
(https://en.wikipedia.org/wiki/Fermat%27s_Last_Theorem#Sophie_Germain)

425.

Bear Grylls survived a free fall parachuting accident from 16,000 feet by landing on his parachuting pack on his back. This crushed three vertebrae but kept him alive.

Reference: (http://www.mailonsunday.co.uk/health/article-450338/Adventurer-Bear-Grylls-battle-pain-high-cholesterol.html)

426.

Founding father and propagandist of the American Revolution, Thomas Paine, wrote a book called "The Age of Reason" arguing against Christianity. He went from a revolutionary hero to reviled, 6 people attended his funeral and 100 years later, Teddy Roosevelt called him a "filthy little atheist".

Reference:
(https://en.wikipedia.org/wiki/The_Age_of_Reason#United_States)

427.

Dogs aren't color blind, but they don't see full color either.

Reference: (http://brightdog.com/dog-vision-see-color-black-white-neither/)

428.

North Korea competed in the 1966 FIFA World Cup in England and got into the knockouts, but lost to Portugal in the Quarterfinals 5-3.

Reference:
(https://en.wikipedia.org/wiki/1966_FIFA_World_Cup#Group_4)

429.

Chewing gum increases cognitive function.

Reference:
(http://www.sciencedirect.com/science/article/pii/S0195666311004703)

430.

France banned an ad depicting Jesus as a female because of its "intrusion on people's innermost beliefs".

Reference: (http://news.bbc.co.uk/2/hi/europe/4337031.stm)

431.

George R. R. Martin wrote in to Marvel about Fantastic Four #17, when he was 12 years old.

Reference: (http://marvel.com/images/911892#0-911892)

432.

In 1973, in New York, a man was arrested for murder. He revealed to his lawyers where 2 other bodies were buried. They withheld the information from police and the families. Vilified at the time, they're now considered heroes for upholding attorney and client privilege.

Reference:
(http://www.abajournal.com/magazine/article/the_toughest_call/)

433.

Jim Henson offered to give 30% of the Muppets to singer and sausage guy Jimmy Dean who wouldn't accept. The stake would have been worth over $200 million when Disney purchased the company.

Reference: (http://www.styleweekly.com/richmond/country-home/Content?oid=2203813)

434.

Although it sank twice in water, the world's oldest paddle steamer is still in timetabled service.

Reference: (https://en.wikipedia.org/wiki/Skibladner)

435.

The "third man factor" is a syndrome that allows certain people to have an unseen presence who provides comfort or support during traumatic experiences.

Reference: (https://en.wikipedia.org/wiki/Third_Man_factor)

436.

The 1st battle between Britain and Germany during World War II took place in South America, it is also the 1st naval battle of World War II.

Reference: (http://www.historylearningsite.co.uk/world-war-two/war-in-the-atlantic/the-battle-of-the-river-plate/)

437.

"New York, New York" by Frank Sinatra was released the same year as "Rappers Delight" by the Sugar Hill Gang.

Reference:
(https://en.wikipedia.org/wiki/Theme_from_New_York,_New_York
)

438.

Anemia or lack of iron can lead to depression.

Reference: (http://www.webmd.com/depression/tc/depression-causes)

439.

The former Australian Prime Minister Bob Hawke was the world record holder for the fastest drinking of a yard of beer, when he drank a sconce pot in eleven seconds as part of a traditional Oxford college penalty.

Reference:
(https://en.wikipedia.org/wiki/Yard_of_ale#Boot_of_beer)

440.

The United States Congress capped the national speed limit at 55 MPH or 88 KMH in response to a fuel shortage and not as a safety precaution.

Reference:
(http://www.nj.gov/transportation/refdata/roadway/speed.shtm)

441.

The Antiques Roadshow appraised a jug to be worth $50,000, comparing it to a Picasso. Unknown to the appraiser, it was actually made by some random high school kid over 40 years ago. After finding out, he changed his appraisal to $5,000, saying it was, "not bad for a high schooler".

Reference: (http://www.pbs.org/wgbh/roadshow/season/20/spokane-wa/appraisals/grotesque-face-jug-ca-1900--201502A19)

442.

Three old frat buddies rigged bets, won $3 million dollars in the 2002 Breeder's Cup, but were caught because they inadvertently bet, and won, on a 43 to 1 longshot.

Reference: (http://articles.baltimoresun.com/2002-11-17/sports/0211170060_1_horse-racing-drexel-polytechnic-institute)

443.

"The Ketchup Song" is a Spanish pop song from 2002. It features a nonsense chorus that is actually comprised of badly distorted lyrics from "Rapper's Delight", heard through the ears of a non-English speaker.

Reference:
(https://en.wikipedia.org/wiki/The_Ketchup_Song_(Aserej%C3%A9)#Content)

444.

There is a chemical called hydrofluoric acid that, even in small concentrations, can cause terrible chemical burns and death due to calcium imbalance. The effects of this acid are not usually evident until a day after exposure.

Reference:
(https://en.wikipedia.org/wiki/Hydrofluoric_acid#Health_and_safety)

445.

A fitness trainer intentionally gained over 70 pounds in order to better understand the plight of his overweight clients. He lost all of it six months later.

Reference: (http://edition.cnn.com/2012/06/05/health/drew-manning-fit2fat2fit-lessons/)

446.

Michael B. Jordan's father is named Michael A. Jordan.

Reference: (https://en.wikipedia.org/wiki/Michael_B._Jordan)

447.

The Watchtower, an illustrated religious magazine distributed by Jehovah's Witnesses, is the most widely circulated magazine in the world, with a print run of 59 million copies bimonthly. It has been distributed free of charge since January, 2000, its printing funded by donations.

Reference: (https://en.wikipedia.org/wiki/The_Watchtower)

448.

Aristotle described the way dolphins sleep in 350 BC.

Reference: (http://pinkmonkey.com/dl/library1/gp007.pdf)

449.

In the 17th century, Johnathan Wild masqueraded as a famous crime-fighter while really being a master criminal.

Reference: (https://en.wikipedia.org/wiki/Jonathan_Wild)

450.

There is a giant grub that, when cooked, tastes like solid bacon.

Reference:
(http://en.wikipedia.org/wiki/Rhynchophorus_ferrugineus#Culinary_uses)

451.

Bolivia has had more coups in its history, above 190, than years that it has been independent for.

Reference: (https://www.loc.gov/rr/frd/cs/profiles/Bolivia.pdf)

452.

The crew of the Doolittle Raid that landed in the Soviet Union were detained due to a neutrality pact. They were later smuggled out by the NKVD.

Reference: (https://en.wikipedia.org/wiki/Doolittle_Raid#Mission)

453.

The first game of softball took place in 1887 and used a balled-up boxing glove as the ball and a broom handle as the bat.

Reference: (https://en.wikipedia.org/wiki/Softball#History)

454.

When Flavor Flav's drug problem was at its worst, he would spend up to $2,600 a day on crack cocaine.

Reference: (https://en.wikipedia.org/wiki/Flavor_Flav)

455.

In 2003, the U.S. Government forcibly seized some 500 horses from two elderly Western Shoshone women on the grounds that they were grazing and destroying "public land". They later found vast deposits of gold, phosphates, and geothermal energy and are now power mining to extract the gold.

Reference: (http://www.frontlinedefenders.org/node/483)

456.

During the 1964 Presidential Election, Barry Goldwater's slogan, "In your heart, you know he's right", was countered by Lyndon B. Johnson's "In your guts, you know he's nuts."

Reference: (https://en.wikipedia.org/wiki/Barry_Goldwater)

457.

The Chinese stole plans for nuclear weapons from the U.S. in 1999.

Reference:(https://en.wikipedia.org/wiki/United_States_Department_of_Energy#Weapon_plans_stolen)

458.

Human Cells contain up to 2 meters of DNA.

Reference: (http://www.ncbi.nlm.nih.gov/books/NBK26834/)

459.

Oprah's TV Network could have rigged a contest against the handicapped internet star Zach Anner.

Reference: (http://www.themarysue.com/zach-anner-rigged-votes-oprah/#geekosystem)

460.

Bono wears sunglasses all the time because he has glaucoma.

Reference: (http://www.theguardian.com/music/2014/oct/17/bono-glaucoma-20-years-u2-dark-glasses)

461.

Seann William Scott's mother likes to go into Best Buy and ask "Do you have American Pie? I'm Stifler's mom".

Reference: (http://metro.co.uk/2015/10/10/20-things-you-didnt-know-about-american-pie-5432726/)

462.

The entire bass linc of the song "Like a G6" is the chord G6.

Reference: (https://tabs.ultimate-guitar.com/f/far_east_movement/like_a_g6_ver5_tab.htm)

463.

The cousin of porn star Lexi Belle found out that she's a porn star while he was masturbating.

Reference: (http://thehundreds.com/blog/porncousin/)

464.

Up until the 1970s, all of the pubs in Ireland were required by law to be closed on St. Patrick's Day.

Reference: (http://www.irishcentral.com/roots/history/All-the-pubs-in-Ireland-used-to-be-closed-on-St-Patricks-Day.html)

465.

For Star Trek's interracial kiss, NBC worried that Southern affiliates might refuse to air the episode, so they filmed the scene with and without the kiss, but stars Nichols and Shatner consciously sabotaged the non-kiss takes so they could only air the kiss version.

Reference: (http://en.memory-alpha.wikia.com/wiki/Nyota_Uhura#James_T._Kirk)

466.

The medieval spice trade involved commodities, like nutmeg, whose origin was unknown to the Europeans and were imported from as far as Indonesia.

Reference: (https://en.wikipedia.org/wiki/Banda_Islands#Pre-European_history)

467.

The global demand for oil is still increasing.

Reference: (https://www.iea.org/oilmarketreport/omrpublic/)

468.

WB Interactive released a DC-world based MOBA, a type of video game, in early 2015 that lasted for 5 months before the servers were shut down.

Reference:
(https://en.wikipedia.org/wiki/Infinite_Crisis_(video_game))

469.

There's a theory that all electrons weigh the same because they are all the same one electron.

Reference: (https://en.wikipedia.org/wiki/One-electron_universe)

470.

A prisoner in the U.S. impregnated 4 guards and made over $15,000 per month while incarcerated.

Reference: (http://www.npr.org/blogs/thetwo-way/2013/04/24/178799235/1-inmate-impregnated-4-guards-at-md-jail-prosecutors-say)

471.

An extremely rare species of tree named Commidendrum rotundifolium grows on a cliff of Saint Helena, the place of exile for Napoleon.

Reference:
(https://en.wikipedia.org/wiki/Commidendrum_rotundifolium)

472.

The Weismann Score was originally invented for the HBO show "Silicon Valley" but is now being used to measure compression ratio and speed.

Reference: (http://spectrum.ieee.org/view-from-the-valley/computing/software/a-madefortv-compression-metric-moves-to-the-real-world)

473.

Bananas are actually a type of berry.

Reference: (http://waynesword.palomar.edu/fruitid1.htm)

474.

The Fedora hat was named after a character in a play called Fedora Romanoff. Sarah Bernhardt, the actress who played her, wore a version of the hat for the role. The name comes from the Greek "theodoros" meaning "gift of God."

Reference: (https://broadly.vice.com/en_us/article/the-history-of-the-fedora)

475.

Ahmad Suradji, an Indonesian serial killer who murdered over 42 women to drink their saliva, believed that it would give him mystic powers as a sorcerer.

Reference:
(http://en.wikipedia.org/wiki/Ahmad_Suradji#coldheartedkilla?)

476.

In the 16th century, Christians called the Anabaptists did not partake in infant baptism, instead believing that only free-willed adults could decide for themselves to be baptized. They were persecuted and killed.

Reference: (https://en.wikipedia.org/wiki/Anabaptists)

477.

The Dover Area School District is known for its students learning intelligent design as an alternative to evolution. This started a case by the parents of the students.

Reference:
(https://en.wikipedia.org/wiki/Kitzmiller_v._Dover_Area_School_District)

478.

The word "Pub" originated as Public House to drink Ale. A "lock-in" is when a pub owner lets drinkers stay in the pub after the legal closing time.

Reference: (https://en.wikipedia.org/wiki/Pub)

479.

Frank Hayes was a jockey who died in 1923 after suffering a fatal heart attack in the middle of a steeplechase at Belmont Park in New York State. His lifeless body stayed on the saddle until his horse crossed the finish line, making him the only jockey known to have won a race after death.

Reference: (http://www.irishmirror.ie/sport/horse-racing/frank-hayes-incredible-story-jockey-5519580)

480.

Martin Pistorious fell into a coma as a young boy. 2 years into his 12 year vegetative state, his conscience was awakened. He was trapped for 10 years in his body, unable to communicate, with only his thoughts for company.

Reference:
(http://www.npr.org/blogs/health/2015/01/09/376084137/trapped-in-his-body-for-12-years-a-man-breaks-free)

481.

The Square Kilometer Array is a radio telescope array that's planned to be built in South Africa and Australia. It will collect so much data that its communication lines will have a capacity greater than all global internet traffic. It will also be 50 times more sensitive than any other radio instrument.

Reference: (https://en.wikipedia.org/wiki/Square_Kilometre_Array)

482.

Takashi Saito, an aspiring 17 year old sumo wrestler, was hazed and beaten with a metal bat by other wrestlers. He died the next day in hospital.

Reference:
(http://www.japantimes.co.jp/news/2009/05/30/national/former-stable-master-gets-six-years-for-young-wrestlers-hazing-death/#.V1lzupErKUn)

483.

Dolphins can get high on puffer fish.

Reference: (http://abcnews.go.com/Technology/dolphins-high-puffer-fish-nature-show/story?id=21385692)

484.

Baffin Island of Canada is nearly twice the size of New Zealand.

Reference: (https://en.wikipedia.org/wiki/Baffin_Island)

485.

Humans are the best on the planet when it comes to long distance running. We can outrun every other animal and run in conditions that no other animal can run in.

Reference: (http://news.harvard.edu/gazette/story/2007/04/humans-hot-sweaty-natural-born-runners/)

486.

One of John F. Kennedy's mistresses plotted to avoid nuclear war by getting J.F.K. to take LSD.

Reference:
(https://en.wikipedia.org/wiki/Mary_Pinchot_Meyer#Timothy_Leary)

487.

Joe Strummer, the lead singer of the Clash, once said he believed that people who aren't adolescents shouldn't make records.

Reference:
(https://en.wikipedia.org/wiki/Graceland_(album)#Release)

488.

The smell of freshly cut grass is actually a plant distress call.

Reference:
(https://www.sciencedaily.com/releases/2014/09/140922145805.htm)

489.

The dictator of Turkmenistan built a 300 meter pillar with a gold topped statue of himself to celebrate the fact that they were neutral.

Reference: (https://en.wikipedia.org/wiki/Neutrality_Monument)

490.

The drinking age in the United States is 21 in an attempt to reduce the risk for alcohol addiction by 90%.

Reference: (http://wait21.org/)

491.

Andre Iguodala interned with Merrill Lynch for a week.

Reference: (https://sports.yahoo.com/news/iguodala-gets-lesson-money-game-201900840--nba.html)

492.

Medieval Europeans believed cotton came from a tree in India that bore tiny lambs on the end of its branches, which bent down for them to feed when they were hungry.

Reference: (https://en.wikipedia.org/wiki/Cotton#Europe)

493.

Anthony Kiedis of the Red Hot Chili Peppers used to be babysat by Sonny and Cher.

Reference: (https://en.wikipedia.org/wiki/Anthony_Kiedis)

494.

The United States Navy tried to blame a deadly 1989 turret explosion on a nonexistent gay love affair between two sailors. Later investigations proved that the explosion was accidental, and caused by problems with the gunpowder bags.

Reference:
(https://en.wikipedia.org/wiki/USS_Iowa_turret_explosion)

495.

The German Parliament building has a glass dome above it that people can walk over. This was done to remind the politicians that the government should be transparent and that the people are always above them.

Reference: (http://en.wikipedia.org/wiki/Reichstag_dome)

496.

Being known as a "No. 8 Wire" in New Zealand is equivalent to a "MacGyver" in the USA.

Reference: (https://en.wikipedia.org/wiki/Number_8_wire)

497.

In Thomas More's Utopia, Utopian couples would see each other naked before they got married on the rationale that a man would not buy a horse before seeing every part of it beforehand.

Reference:(http://www.bl.uk/learning/histcitizen/21cc/utopia/more1/engagement1/engagement.html)

498.

Moses is mentioned more times in the Qur'an than the Prophet Mohammed.

Reference: (http://www.bibleodyssey.org/en/people/related-articles/moses-and-the-quran.aspx)

499.

A British Airways flight was forced to turn around after 30 minutes in the air because of bad smelling feces.

Reference: (http://www.bbc.co.uk/newsbeat/article/31908620/ba-flight-forced-to-land-early-because-of-smelly-poo)

500.

Around 1880, there was a mining town in California that was so nefarious that, upon learning her family was moving there, one girl wrote in her diary, "Goodbye God, I'm going to Bodie."

Reference: (http://www.desertusa.com/bodie/bodie.html)

501.

It takes 75,000 trees to print a Sunday edition of the New York Times.

Reference: (https://www.usi.edu/recycle/paper-recycling-facts)

502.

The first streaming music service started in 1897. Users in New York could pick up their phones and connect to the Telharmonium, which was a central hub that would pipe music being played live by two musicians playing 24 hours a day.

Reference: (http://www.atlasobscura.com/articles/the-telharmonium-was-the-spotify-of-1906)

503.

An Indian rationalist was accused of blasphemy and had to flee the country after he proved that the "miracle" tears coming from a Jesus statue actually came from clogged drainage pipes. The man who offered him safety if he came back, was murdered.

Reference: (http://www.theguardian.com/world/2012/nov/23/india-blasphemy-jesus-tears)

504.

A decade before the SR-71 first flew, the Military had a Mach 4.3 capable Ramjet created to test its own air defenses. It was so effective that it was cancelled to avoid embarrassing the military's own air defenses any further. The man who designed it went on to create the SR-71 spy plane.

Reference: (https://en.wikipedia.org/wiki/Lockheed_AQM-60_Kingfisher)

505.

Bob Ross never received any money for his show, The Joy of Painting. His company, Bob Ross Inc., sold art supplies, how to videos and he gave art lessons.

Reference: (http://mentalfloss.com/article/23260/5-happy-little-things-you-didnt-know-about-bob-ross)

506.

There is a city in Turkey named Batman, whose former mayor sued Chris Nolan for the unauthorized use of the city's name in "The Dark Knight."

Reference: (https://en.wikipedia.org/wiki/H%C3%BCseyin_Kalkan)

507.

The serial killer with the most victims, possibly over 400, was only sentenced to 30 years in jail.

Reference: (http://en.wikipedia.org/wiki/Luis_Garavito#Sentencing)

508.

The Republican Party was formed to oppose slavery.

Reference: (https://en.wikipedia.org/wiki/History_of_the_United_States_Republican_Party)

509.

A man in San Francisco declared himself the, "Emperor of America and Protector of Mexico." The people were such good sports about it that they honored his regal decrees and the currency that he created was widely accepted around the city. When he died, 30,000 people attended his funeral.

Reference: (https://en.wikipedia.org/wiki/Emperor_Norton)

510.

When bubbles are collapsed by sound waves it creates light and no one really knows why. The phenomena is called "sonoluminescence."

Reference: (https://en.wikipedia.org/wiki/Sonoluminescence)

511.

In 2015, a bus driver in India took a nap on his bus, only to be awoken to a monkey that had climbed into the driver's cabin and had started the engine. As the driver ran to the cabin, the monkey panicked, shifted gears and jumped out. The bus rammed 2 other buses before the driver regained control.

Reference:
(http://timesofindia.indiatimes.com/city/bareilly/Monkey-drives-bus-rams-it-into-2-other-vehicles/articleshow/50286858.cms)

512.

Between 2004 and 2006, more than 500 Indian workers were lured into working for shipyards in America with the promise of American citizenship. The company sent them into a labor camp, held their passports, extorted them with lies about various fees, and threatened them with legal and physical harm.

Reference: (https://www.aclu.org/human-rights/david-et-al-v-signal-international-llc-et-al)

513.

Japanese professional sumo wrestlers are banned from driving by the association because some are just too big to fit behind a steering wheel and if they drove, it could lead to a serious car accident.

Reference:
(https://en.wikipedia.org/wiki/Sumo#Life_as_a_professional_sumo_wrestler)

514.

Bob Marley had 3 children born to 3 different women in one month.

Reference:
(http://en.wikipedia.org/wiki/Bob_Marley#Final_years_and_death)

515.

After Congressman, John Rankin, refused to sit next to Adam Clayton Powell Jr. because of the color of his skin, Powell found every opportunity possible to sit close to the Mississippi Congressman. On one occasion, Powell followed him from seat to seat until Rankin had moved five times.

Reference: (http://www.greatblackheroes.com/government/adam-clayton-powell-jr/)

516.

Another word for "flinching" is "blenching."

Reference: (http://www.merriam-webster.com/dictionary/blench)

517.

Ronald L. Sanford is currently serving a 170 year sentence for a double homicide and robbery that he committed in 1987, at the age of 13.

Reference: (http://www.scribes.eu/2013/01/ronald-l-sanford-170-years-in-indiana_23.html)

518.

The commonly agreed upon number of aerial takedowns to become an ace pilot is 5, and the most recent American aviator to become an ace pilot did so in 1972.

Reference:(https://en.wikipedia.org/wiki/Flying_ace#Afghanistan_in
vasion.2C_Global_War_on_Terrorism_.282001.E2.80.93present.29)

519.

There is an orange type specifically for juicing and an orange type specifically for eating.

Reference: (http://fruitguys.com/almanac/2012/05/21/navels-vs-valencias)

520.

The Japanese honey bee defends their hive from the Japanese giant hornet by creating a convection oven around the hornet. The bees surround the hornet in a ball containing around 500 in number, vibrating their wings and heating the air inside the ball to 117 degrees Fahrenheit.

Reference: (https://en.wikipedia.org/wiki/Japanese_giant_hornet)

521.

The high visibility markings on British emergency vehicles are called Battenburg markings, due to their resemblance to the Battenberg cake.

Reference:
(https://en.wikipedia.org/wiki/Battenburg_markings?repost)

522.

Andrew Garfield was fired from Sony's Spiderman franchise because he didn't show up to a Sony Gala Dinner.

Reference: (http://www.ibtimes.co.uk/real-reason-behind-andrew-garfield-getting-fired-sonys-spider-man-franchise-revealed-1499428)

523.

A woman walked across the United States continuously for 28 years, only to be killed in an automobile accident while being driven to a speaking engagement about her travels.

Reference:
(https://en.wikipedia.org/wiki/Peace_Pilgrim#Pilgrimage)

524.

Show producers gave a homeless man $100,000 to do what he wants with; within 6 months he had nearly spent all the money and he eventually went broke and became homeless again.

Reference:
(http://en.wikipedia.org/wiki/Reversal_of_Fortune_%282005_film%29)

525.

In darkness, most people will eventually adjust to a 48 hour cycle. This includes 36 hours of activity followed by 12 hours of sleep. The reasons behind this are still unclear.

Reference: (http://www.bbc.com/future/story/20140514-how-extreme-isolation-warps-minds)

526.

Britain became an island after the English Channel was carved out from 2 megafloods caused by the melting of a large ice sheet that covered Britain and Scandinavia 450,000 years ago.

Reference:
(http://www.forbes.com/sites/shaenamontanari/2016/02/06/the-english-channel-megaflood-and-how-britain-became-an-island/#63f8bade8389)

527.

When Steve Jobs refused to give early Apple employees stock, Steve Wozniak offered them $10 million worth of his.

Reference: (http://www.businessinsider.com/steve-wozniak-gave-early-apple-employees-10-million-in-stock-2014-9)

528.

The Phantom Time Hypothesis states that the years A.D. 614 to 911 never actually happened and that we're currently living in the 18th century.

Reference: (https://www.youtube.com/watch?v=i7V0LIxHtt8)

529.

Treasury Secretary Jack Lew had to change his signature to make it more legible on U.S. currency.

Reference: (https://www.washingtonpost.com/news/wonk/wp/2013/06/18/jack-lews-new-signature-unveiled/)

530.

You can get a Dr. Pepper and other corporate brands as personalized license plates in Texas.

Reference: (http://www.myplates.com/Personalized/PLPC183)

531.

Because of the frequency and massive destruction cause by hail in Alberta, insurance companies pay for cloud seeding planes that spray silver iodine to make the rain fall before it becomes hail.

Reference: (http://www.canadiangeographic.ca/magazine/ja98/feature_hailstorms.asp)

532.

Ruth Coker Burks, also known as the Cemetery Angel, took in over 40 AIDS patients when their families turned them away.

Reference: (http://www.arktimes.com/arkansas/ruth-coker-burks-the-cemetery-angel/Content?oid=3602959)

533.

Catullus' Carmen 16 is a poem so dirty that it wasn't fully translated into English until the late 20th century, despite being almost 2000 years old.

Reference: (http://io9.gizmodo.com/a-latin-poem-so-filthy-it-wasnt-translated-until-the-2-1589504370)

534.

In the 19th century, doctors would "cure" a woman suffering from hysteria by administering a vaginal massage until the woman had an orgasm; this practice led to the invention of the vibrator for "home practice."

Reference: (http://en.wikipedia.org/wiki/Female_hysteria)

535.

Fake cell towers, called Stingrays, are used by law enforcement to trick cell phones into giving GPS and identifying info. When used to track a suspect, it also fathers information of all cellphones nearby.

Reference: (https://www.aclu.org/node/37337)

536.

Baseball prospect Matt Harrington was selected in the MLB draft five times in consecutive years, without coming to an agreement. He now puts tires on cars for $11.50 per hour.

Reference: (https://en.wikipedia.org/wiki/Matt_Harrington)

537.

A man became stranded in the woods after his canoe capsized near shore. Possessing only an axe, he cut power poles to draw attention and the repair crew in northern Saskatchewan came to his rescue.

Reference:
(http://www.cbc.ca/beta/news/canada/saskatchewan/stranded-man-cuts-power-poles-to-draw-attention-1.890115)

538.

The United States military has more aircraft than the next 7 countries combined.

Reference: (http://www.globalfirepower.com/aircraft-total.asp)

539.

Vernors is actually the oldest soda still being sold. It predates Dr. Pepper by 19 years.

Reference: (http://en.wikipedia.org/w/index.php?title=Vernors)

540.

In the DC universe, Santa Claus is a powerful 1800 year old immortal entity whose bone dust was once snorted like cocaine by John Constantine.

Reference: (http://dc.wikia.com/wiki/Santa_Claus)

541.

Natalie Dormer has a Dune inspired tattoo.

Reference:
(http://www.esquire.com/entertainment/tv/a25124/natalie-dormer-tattoo/)

542.

In 1970, a group of hikers outside of Bergen, Norway, suddenly came upon the charred, naked, fingerprint-less corpse of a woman in the middle of the Isdalen Valley. The woman was nicknamed the Isdal Woman and her story remains one of Norway's deepest mysteries.

Reference: (https://en.wikipedia.org/wiki/Isdal_Woman)

543.

Christopher Nolan doesn't own a mobile phone or have an email address.

Reference: (http://www.hollywoodreporter.com/news/dark-knight-rises-christopher-nolan-batman-352120)

544.

ASIMO, the world's most advanced humanoid robot, can run up to 5 MPH, walk up and down stairs, jump on one foot, dance, play soccer and serve drinks.

Reference: (https://www.youtube.com/watch?v=sKdYIPPeK-Q&feature=youtu.be)

545.

On September 11th, 2006, Russia gifted the United States a memorial for the 911 attacks and the 1993 World Trade Center bombing.

Reference: (http://www.911monument.com/)

546.

Joe DiMaggio had 361 career home runs and only struck out 369 times in 13 years.

Reference: (http://www.baseball-reference.com/players/d/dimagjo01.shtml)

547.

The 4 colors used in the PlayStation logo stand for Brilliance, Passion, Joy and Charm.

Reference: (http://famouslogos.net/playstation-logo/)

548.

The Curonians are a nearly extinct Baltic ethnic group. They live on the Curonian Spit, a 98 kilometer long, thin, curve sand-dune spit which is shared between Latvia and Lithuania.

Reference: (https://en.wikipedia.org/wiki/Kursenieki)

549.

President Grover Cleveland avoided the draft by paying a Polish immigrant to fight in his place during the Civil War.

Reference:
(https://en.wikipedia.org/wiki/Grover_Cleveland#Early_career_and_the_Civil_War)

550.

A good brakeman, a railroad worker who coupled trains, in the late 1800s was often missing a few fingers, otherwise they were considered a green horn.

Reference: (https://web.stanford.edu/group/spatialhistory/cgi-bin/site/pub.php?id=65)

551.

A female cat can have kittens until they die of old age. Only we and 2 other species have menopause.

Reference: (http://www.livescience.com/22574-animals-menopause.html)

552.

There's a company you can send your feces to that will sequence and analyze your gut bacteria for under $100.

Reference: (http://blogs.discovermagazine.com/crux/2015/10/07/poop-sample-ubiome/)

553.

One-Eyed Frank McGee, an early Ottawa hockey player who lost his sight in one eye playing the sport, cheated on the vision test required to join the military during World War I by switching hands instead of eyes.

Reference: (http://www.thecanadianencyclopedia.ca/en/article/frank-mcgee/)

554.

Human–animal breastfeeding, women breastfeeding young animals, or animals breastfeeding human children, such as goats, has been practiced throughout history.

Reference: (http://factday.com/2012/05/25/some-women-breastfeeding-animals/)

555.

In 2011, a man shot a high powered rifle at the White House. He hit it at least 7 times and it took the Secret Service 4 days to realize that the house had even been hit. They only realized after a housekeeper noticed that there was broken glass and cement on the floor.

Reference: (http://www.washingtonpost.com/politics/secret-service-stumbled-after-gunman-hit-white-house-residence-in-

2011/2014/09/27/d176b6ac-442a-11e4-b437-
1a7368204804_story.html)

556.

People who have friends live longer than those without.

Reference: (http://www.livescience.com/6769-live-longer-
friends.html)

557.

On May 30th, 1883, a woman tripped on the Brooklyn Bridge,
sparking panic that the bridge was collapsing. The resulting
stampede ended with 12 people dead and more than 35 wounded.

Reference: (http://untappedcities.com/2013/10/23/rumor-brooklyn-
bridge-stampede-collapse-sparked-fatal-during-opening-week/)

558.

Eminem was asked to star in the 2013 film "Elysium," but turned it
down because the director wouldn't set the movie in Detroit.

Reference:
(http://www.theguardian.com/music/2013/jul/18/eminem-di-
antwoord-ninja-elysium)

559.

As a way of thanking the doctors that looked after his seriously ill
daughter, Johnny Depp visited the Great Ormond Street Hospital in
London and read stories to sick kids for over four hours in full Jack
Sparrow attire.

Reference:
(http://en.wikipedia.org/wiki/Johnny_Depp#Family_and_relationshi
ps)

560.

There is a company that will preserve your tattoo after you die via a taxidermy process.

Reference: (http://www.wallsandskin.com/preserveyourtattoos/)

561.

Johnny Depp's last name means "fool" in German.

Reference: (https://www.dict.cc/?s=Depp)

562.

In 2001, British author Giles Foden, best known for his novel "Last King of Scotland", compared Eminem to Robert Browning, one of the foremost Victorian poets. Foden remarked that a "brief examination of "Stan" reveals it to have all the depth and texture of the greatest examples of English verse."

Reference: (http://usatoday30.usatoday.com/life/music/news/2011-02-04-eminembard04_ST_N.htm)

563.

Japanese death row inmates aren't told their date of execution. They wake up each day wondering if today may be their last day.

Reference: (http://japanfocus.org/-David-McNeill/2402/article.html)

564.

During the Nazi occupation of France, Hitler did not destroy the Canadian Vimy Memorial and told the Allies that it remained intact. He did this because he admired the peaceful nature of the sculpture.

Reference:
(http://en.wikipedia.org/wiki/Canadian_National_Vimy_Memorial)

565.

There is a gypsy tribe in India that celebrates death as one of the happiest events in their lives, while treating births as occasions of great grief.

Reference: (http://www.dnaindia.com/india/report-rajasthans-gypsy-tribe-celebrate-death-mourn-births-1732138)

566.

Motor neuron disease has been on the increase for over ten years, and scientists think pesticides, pollutants and paints are to blame.

Reference:
(http://www.theguardian.com/uk/2004/aug/15/health.healthandwellbeing)

567.

A team of developers is taking the glow in the dark enzyme that is in certain jellyfish and fireflies and is creating bioluminescent trees. These trees can potentially light up public streets while being energy neutral.

Reference: (http://www.huffingtonpost.com/2014/03/30/daan-roosegaarde_n_5044578.html)

568.

In 2004, a woman died on a pendulum ride due to negligence. Afterwards, the park manager was convicted of reckless homicide.

Reference: (http://www.cnn.com/2005/LAW/05/17/ctv.martin/)

569.

The sand on Uranus is as fine as smoke molecules.

Reference:(http://www.nasa.gov/audience/foreducators/postsecondary/features/F_Planet_Seasons.html)

570.

Bryan Ware recycles crayons from restaurants that would have been otherwise thrown away. He then takes these child friendly crayons and gives them to hospitals.

Reference: (http://www.barnorama.com/bryan-ware-knows-how-to-reuse-leftover-crayons-from-restaurants-and-schools/)

571.

Hitler sanctioned the construction of a six-wheeled 3,000 horsepower Porsche intended to break the land speed record. It was 27 feet long and made its power from a 44.5 liter V12 engine.

Reference: (https://en.wikipedia.org/wiki/Mercedes-Benz_T80)

572.

In 1255, King Henry III of England received an elephant from King Louis IX of France. It died in 1257 from drinking too much red wine.

Reference:
(https://en.wikipedia.org/wiki/History_of_elephants_in_Europe)

573.

Wanz, or the "deep voice" in the song "Thrift Shop" was a full-time software engineer prior to its release. In 2015, he again took up a full-time job as a quality-assurance engineer at a software company.

Reference: (https://en.wikipedia.org/wiki/Wanz)

574.

There is an actual index for perceived national corruption and the U.S. doesn't even make the top 20.

Reference:
(http://en.wikipedia.org/wiki/Corruption_Perceptions_Index)

575.

More than half of Israel's water consumption relies on artificial water supplies.

Reference: (http://www.businessinsider.com/israel-style-methods-arent-going-to-solve-californias-devastating-drought-2015-6)

576.

The Kohler Design Center is the Kohler Company museum showcase of product design in Kohler, Wisconsin. It features Kohler's own "Great Wall of China," which is a floor-to-ceiling display of toilets.

Reference: (http://www.us.kohler.com/us/Main-Level:-Product-Pavilion-&-Water-Deck/content/CNT400057.htm)

577.

Vox Media, the corporation behind Vox, The Verge, Polygon and Re/code, is financially backed by Comcast's venture capital fund.

Reference: (https://en.wikipedia.org/wiki/Vox_Media)

578.

Florence Nightingale, the quintessential English nurse, was born in Florence, Italy.

Reference: (https://en.wikipedia.org/wiki/Florence_Nightingale)

579.

When Eddie Murphy was on SNL in the early 1980s, other cast members often had to go downstairs after shows to catch a cab for him because no cab drivers would stop for a young black man late at night.

Reference:(http://books.google.ca/books?id=3Qx0AwAAQBAJ&lpg=PT219&ots=pr3qwNKyam&dq=eddie+murphy+cabs+won%27t+stop+live+from+new+york&pg=PT220&redir_esc=y#v=onepage&q&f=false)

580.

When a skydiver, Joan Murray's, parachute failed to open, she fell to the ground at 80 miles per hour. She landed on a mound of fire ants which began to sting her. The shock of being stung over 200 times by the fire ants released a surge of adrenaline which kept her heart beating and allowed her to survive.

Reference:
(http://en.wikipedia.org/wiki/Joan_Murray_%28skydiver%29)

581.

The first rap song to top number 1 on Billboard charts was Blondie's "Rapture", sung by Debbie Harry, a white female. It was also the first rap music video to appear on MTV.

Reference: (https://en.wikipedia.org/wiki/Rapture_(Blondie_song))

582.

In 19th century France, stereoscopes of Hell were popular.

Reference: (http://www.londonstereo.com/diableries/index.html)

583.

Police in the Chinese city of Shenzhen have come up with a novel "eye for an eye" method of punishing drivers who misuse their headlights and dazzle other road users. Anyone doing so will be made to stare at the police's own full beam headlights for five minutes.

Reference: (http://www.independent.co.uk/news/world/asia/chinese-drivers-forced-to-stare-at-fullbeam-headlights-in-eye-for-an-eye-punishment-for-those-who-dazzle-others-9659736.html)

584.

A tax auditor in Finland died at his desk, and despite there being 100 staff on the same floor in the department no-one realized he was dead for 2 days.

Reference: (http://news.bbc.co.uk/1/hi/world/europe/3410547.stm)

585.

From the 1600s to the 1920s, doctors routinely aided in female masturbation sessions to "cure hysteria."

Reference: (https://www.nytimes.com/books/first/m/maines-technology.html)

586.

A "billion" in England was defined as a million million, up until 1974.

Reference: (https://en.wikipedia.org/wiki/Long_and_short_scales)

587.

The "Miss Cleo free tarot reading" psychic hotline was generating $24 million a month for two years straight. Miss Cleo herself only earned $1,750 for the three days it took to film the first infomercial.

Reference: (http://www.vice.com/read/we-spoke-to-ms-cleo-about-her-fake-patois-and-getting-ripped-off-by-her-old-bosses)

588.

The ZIP in ZIP Code stands for Zone Improvement Plan.

Reference: (https://en.wikipedia.org/wiki/ZIP_code)

589.

Japan planned to wage biological warfare on the Californian civilian population centers during World War II, through the use of the flea plague.

Reference:
(https://en.wikipedia.org/wiki/Operation_Cherry_Blossoms_at_Night)

590.

Mary Fields, a 6 foot, 200 pound former slave became the second woman and the first African American to work for the U.S. Postal Service in Montana. She began to work for the USPS at the age of 60 after hitching a team of six horses faster than any cowboy and never missed work in 10 years.

Reference: (http://en.wikipedia.org/wiki/Mary_Fields)

591.

As a teenager, Benjamin Franklin was published under the pseudonym, Mrs. Silence Dogood, a middle-aged widow.

Reference: (http://writerscircle.com/whats-in-a-name-5-authors-and-their-pseudonyms-2/?utm_source=twc-twcfan&utm_medium=social-fb&utm_term=20160411&utm_content=link&utm_campaign=whats-in-a-name-5-authors-and-their-pseudonyms-2&origin=twc_twcfan_social_fb_link_whats-in-a-name-5-authors-and-their-pseudonyms-2_20160411)

592.

A child growing up in the U.S. is more likely to have a pet than a live-at-home father.

Reference: (http://www.americanhumane.org/interaction/support-the-bond/fact-sheets/animal-abuse-domestic-violence.html)

593.

The oldest known joke is a Sumerian fart joke.

Reference: (http://goodmenproject.com/featured-content/from-the-sumerians-to-shakespeare-to-twain-why-fart-jokes-never-get-old-wcz/)

594.

Carl Sagan insisted that it was common practice for NASA astronauts to be given cyanide pills in-case they could not return to Earth.

Reference: (http://en.wikipedia.org/wiki/Suicide_pill)

595.

Weird Al Yankovic lost both of his parents to carbon monoxide poisoning from their fireplace.

Reference:
(https://en.wikipedia.org/wiki/%22Weird_Al%22_Yankovic#Personal_life)

596.

Singer Rod Stewart is deeply into model railroads and has even been on the cover of Model Railroader Magazine.

Reference:
(https://en.wikipedia.org/wiki/Rod_Stewart#Personal_life)

597.

A convicted murderer escaped 3 times from a federal prison, once by mailing himself out in a crate.

Reference: (https://en.wikipedia.org/wiki/Richard_Lee_McNair)

598.

The National Geographic Society was founded by Alexander Graham Bell's father-in-law. Bell succeeded him as President in 1897 and Bell's son-in-law in turn became the first full-time editor of the magazine in 1899.

Reference:
(https://en.wikipedia.org/wiki/National_Geographic_Society#History)

599.

Some heroin addicts, once free of their addiction, continue to inject water into their veins.

Reference: (https://www.vice.com/en_uk/read/heroin-addicts-who-cant-inject-heroin-238)

600.

Dr. Robert Liston is the only known surgeon with a 300% mortality rate in a single operation.

Reference: (http://mentalfloss.com/article/31514/table-one-history%E2%80%99s-most-infamous-surgeons)

601.

Meher Baba, an Indian spiritual master, didn't speak for the last 44 years of his life.

Reference: (https://en.wikipedia.org/wiki/Meher_Baba)

602.

Apple released their first tablet computer, the Newton, in 1993.

Reference: (http://www.goexplore.net/future-tech/12-technology-fails-ahead-of-their-time/)

603.

Researchers created an "MIT science club for disabled children" then fed the children radioactive cereal to help Quaker Oats prove that their product was more nutritious than their competitor, Cream of Wheat. They told the children that they were eating vitamins and would get baseball tickets.

Reference: (http://priceonomics.com/the-mit-science-club-for-disabled-children/)

604.

France had its own calendar for only 12 years starting in 1792. Each week had 10 days, each day 10 hours, each hour 100 minutes, and each minute 100 seconds.

Reference:
(http://en.wikipedia.org/wiki/French_Republican_Calendar)

605.

A woman in Ohio was sentenced to spend a night in the woods without food, water or entertainment because she abandoned 35 kittens.

Reference:
(http://abcnews.go.com/GMA/LegalCenter/story?id=1322751#.UOx Y56RYsqY)

606.

When Merle Haggard was nine years old, his mother got him violin lessons. However, the teacher said that it was a waste of her money because he had too good of an ear to learn how to read music as he could already play something he heard on the radio.

Reference:
(http://www.esquire.com/entertainment/interviews/a3315/whativelea
rned0907/)

607.

When New York City Hall was renovated in 1903, a secret stairwell was discovered. It was said to be used by aldermen to escape the building when angry constituents were waiting for them outside.

Reference: (http://cdnc.ucr.edu/cgi-
bin/cdnc?a=d&d=LAH19030731.2.20)

608.

The longest time a pair of twins have been born apart is 87 days.

Reference: (http://www.mirror.co.uk/news/real-life-stories/miracle-
twins-born-record-87-1857782)

609.

An all-female Soviet regiment, nicknamed the "night witches," would fly thousands of feet up and cut their engines to drop bombs on German forces undetected.

Reference: (http://www.vanityfair.com/culture/2015/06/night-
witches-wwii-female-pilots)

610.

Some parents give their kids bleach enemas up their rectum in hope of curing them of diseases and conditions such as autism.

Reference: (http://www.vice.com/en_ca/read/parents-are-giving-
their-children-bleach-enemas-to-cure-them-of-autism-311)

611.

The man who wrote the Chili's baby back ribs jingle wrote it in five minutes and besides for making $2,000 dollars for it appearing in Austin Powers, hasn't made any money from it since.

Reference: (https://munchies.vice.com/en/articles/the-inventor-of-the-chilis-baby-back-ribs-song-has-never-eaten-their-ribs)

612.

The United States Missile Defense Agency is planning to put electric lasers on UAVs to bring down fighters and anti-aircraft missiles.

Reference: (http://breakingdefense.com/2015/08/return-of-the-abl-missile-defense-agency-works-on-laser-drone/)

613.

The magnitude 9.0 great earthquake that struck Japan on March 11th, 2011, was so powerful that its rumble was "heard" from space. Scientists in France and the Netherlands have found that sound waves from the quake reached as far as an orbiting satellite, 260 kilometers above.

Reference: (http://www.nature.com/news/earthquake-detected-from-space-1.12545)

614.

The upper balconies of American churches and theaters were once commonly referred to as "Nigger Heaven".

Reference:
(http://en.wikipedia.org/wiki/Nigger_Heaven#Background)

615.

In 2011, a study found that individuals with high social anxiety had high empathy. The study found that high empathy may makes socially anxious individuals more sensitive and attentive to other people's states of mind.

Reference: (http://www.ncbi.nlm.nih.gov/pubmed/22120444)

616.

Carrie Nation would attack alcohol-serving establishments with a hatchet.

Reference: (https://en.wikipedia.org/wiki/Carrie_Nation#.22Hatchetations.22)

617.

MMA journalist, Rafael Torre, faked his BJJ credentials, lied his way into MMA inner circles, and was convicted of murder for choking to death the husband of a woman that he was having an affair with during BJJ instruction.

Reference: (http://www.sherdog.com/news/news/Torre-Guilty-of-Murder-Prosecution-Wont-Seek-Death-Penalty-3275)

618.

Dandelions aren't native to the America's.

Reference: (http://invasivore.org/2011/05/species-profile-common-dandelion-taraxacum-officinale/)

619.

Even though whales don't have external earlobes, they still make earwax. An adult whale can have two foot-long columns of wax in their head, and scientists can harvest them to learn more about what chemicals the whales were exposed to throughout their life.

Reference: (http://www.npr.org/2013/09/17/223139796/ear-wax-from-whales-keeps-record-of-ocean-contaminants)

620.

Foreign Accent Syndrome is a speech disorder that causes the person to start speaking with a foreign accent from a country that they've never visited. This happens when the person suffers a traumatic brain injury.

Reference: (https://www.utdallas.edu/research/FAS/about/)

621.

Glitches in apps designed to track stolen phones sent over a dozen people, sometimes accompanied by police, to an innocent couple's Atlanta home. The phones are from different manufacturers and server carriers; the involved companies, and even the FCC, claim that they can do nothing about it.

Reference: (http://www.mnn.com/green-tech/gadgets-electronics/blogs/house-atlanta-keeps-stealing-peoples-iphones?utm_source=fark&utm_medium=website&utm_content=link)

622.

With over 1600 volcanoes, Venus has more volcanoes than any other planet in the solar system.

Reference: (http://volcano.oregonstate.edu/oldroot/volcanoes/planet_volcano/venus/intro.html)

623.

Compared with a single cigarette, one hookah session delivers approximately 2.5 times the nicotine, 25 times the tar, 125 times the smoke and 10 times the carbon monoxide.

Reference: (http://www.mensfitness.com/life/entertainment/hookah-packs-25-times-tar-single-cigarette)

624.

Singapore got expelled from Malaysia.

Reference:
(https://en.wikipedia.org/wiki/Singapore#Merger_with_Malaysia)

625.

In 1969, the United States, under Richard Nixon, went into a nuclear readiness alert and flew nuclear armed bombers along Soviet airspace for three days. This was part of Nixon's "Madman Theory," in which he tried to give off the image that he was unstable so that Soviet bloc nations would never provoke the United States.

Reference: (https://en.wikipedia.org/wiki/Madman_theory)

626.

The ATMs in Vatican City are in Latin.

Reference: (http://gizmodo.com/5905595/the-atms-in-vatican-city-speak-latin)

627.

Diet Coke is the same formula as New Coke but with no sugar.

Reference:
(https://en.wikipedia.org/wiki/New_Coke#Company_dissatisfaction)

628.

96% of employers in New Hampshire are small business owners.

Reference: (http://www.movoto.com/guide/nh/new-hampshire-facts/)

629.

The first victim of the September 11th backlash was a Sikh by the name of Balbir Singh Sodhi. He was shot dead at a gas station in Mesa, Arizona.

Reference:
(https://en.wikipedia.org/wiki/Murder_of_Balbir_Singh_Sodhi)

630.

Over 5,000 Amish people travel each year to a place in Pinecraft, Florida called the "Amish Las Vegas". The use of cell phones and cameras is very common there and almost everyone uses electricity in their rental homes.

Reference: (http://www.nytimes.com/2012/04/15/travel/pinecraft-fla-an-amish-snowbird-magnet.html?_r=0)

631.

The last true battle to occur on English soil was the Clifton Moor Skirmish, which took place in 1745.

Reference: (https://en.wikipedia.org/wiki/Clifton_Moor_Skirmish)

632.

There exists a massive abandoned supercollider in Texas.

Reference: (http://sometimes-interesting.com/2012/01/31/worlds-largest-super-collider-abandoned/#more-2259)

633.

Your brain treats LEGO people as if they're alive.

Reference: (http://digest.bps.org.uk/2016/02/your-brain-treats-lego-people-as-if.html)

634.

Jaguars eat a vine called Yage to induce a hallucinogenic state that heightens its senses and makes it extremely "high".

Reference: (https://www.youtube.com/watch?v=OqGDv0KCJl8)

635.

The United States is currently withholding over 5,000 patents and inventions in the interests of National Security.

Reference: (https://www.law.cornell.edu/uscode/text/35/part-II/chapter-17)

636.

A man built a secret apartment at a mall, and got away with it for four years.

Reference: (https://consumerist.com/2007/10/03/man-builds-secret-apartment-at-mall-gets-away-with-it-for-four-years/)

637.

Citizens of Russia can legally identify as any ethnicity, real or not. According to official statistics in the 2002 census, there are Russian citizens who identify as Babylonians, Romans, Martians, Goblins, Elves and Hobbits.

Reference: (http://en.wikipedia.org/wiki/Russian_Census_(2002))

638.

There are ponds and lakes in Antarctica that, despite year round frozen temperatures, never freeze due to their salt content.

Reference: (https://en.wikipedia.org/wiki/Don_Juan_Pond)

639.

The most valuable vinyl record of all time is not a rare recording, it's a plain, off the shelf, version of Double Fantasy by John Lennon and Yoko Ono. It's worth half a million dollars because John Lennon signed the cover for Mark David Chapman 5 hours before Chapman murdered Lennon.

Reference: (http://www.biography.com/people/mark-david-chapman-9244472#synopsis)

640.

When Anglerfish mate, they melt into each other and share their bodies forever. If a male finds a female, he latches on and fuses to her, losing his internal organs until they share a bloodstream.

Reference:
(http://animals.nationalgeographic.com/animals/fish/anglerfish)

641.

Between 1988 and 1997, Taco Bell's main slogan was "Make a Run for The Border!"

Reference: (http://slogans.wikia.com/wiki/Taco_Bell)

642.

If people in the 10% for alcohol consumption were to reduce their total consumption to that of the next lowest 10% group; alcohol sales would drop by 60% in the U.S.

Reference:
(http://www.washingtonpost.com/blogs/wonkblog/wp/2014/09/25/think-you-drink-a-lot-this-chart-will-tell-you/)

643.

An Olympic rower stopped mid race to let a family of ducks pass. And still won.

Reference:
(http://en.wikipedia.org/wiki/Bobby_Pearce_%28sculler%29)

644.

The first Saab dealership in the United States was opened and managed by Kurt Vonnegut.

Reference: (http://www.saabhistory.com/2007/04/15/saab-cape-cod-kurt-vonneguts-dealership/)

645.

John Odom is a professional baseball player whose team traded him for 10 bats. Odom later died from a heroin overdose.

Reference: (https://en.wikipedia.org/wiki/John_Odom_(baseball))

646.

Nickelback was the second best-selling foreign act in the U.S. of the 2000s, behind The Beatles at number one.

Reference: (https://en.wikipedia.org/wiki/Nickelback)

647.

A hummingbird weighs less than a penny.

Reference: (http://animals.mom.me/weight-hummingbird-3660.html)

648.

In the year 40, two sisters in Vietnam led a rebellion which resulted in the Chinese getting kicked out of Vietnam for three years.

Reference: (https://en.wikipedia.org/wiki/Trung_sisters%27_rebellion)

649.

On the 50th anniversary of the adoption of the Declaration of Independence, longtime friends and rivals, John Adams and Thomas Jefferson, both died, unaware of the other's death.

Reference: (https://en.wikipedia.org/wiki/John_Adams#Death)

650.

The actors who played R2-D2 and C-3PO on "Star Wars", hated each other. The man who played C-3PO once told the other man, "I don't do many of these conventions - go away little man," when he was asked to go on tour.

Reference: (http://gizmodo.com/the-men-inside-of-r2-d2-and-c-3po-actually-hated-each-o-1571528684)

651.

Comcast tried to buy the Walt Disney Company in 2004 for a total of $66 billion dollars.

Reference:(https://en.wikipedia.org/wiki/Comcast#Largest_US_cable_provider_.282001.E2.80.93present.29)

652.

In 2011, scientists at UC Berkeley were able to reconstruct images seen by a patient by scanning their brain with an MRI scan and running the data through a program.

Reference:(https://www.youtube.com/watch?v=6FsH7RK1S2E&feature=youtu.be&ab_channel=UCBerkeley)

653.

The Royal College of Surgeons in London houses a museum that displays thousands of anatomical specimens including human heads, limbs, organs, and the skeleton of the "Irish Giant" Charles Byrne.

Reference: (http://www.rcseng.ac.uk/museums/hunterian/about-us/collections.html)

654.

Apollo 11 astronauts had to declare moon rocks through customs upon their return to Earth.

Reference: (http://www.space.com/7044-moon-apollo-astronauts-customs.html)

655.

Ernest Hemingway begged his wife not to send him for more electroshock treatments because he lost so much of his memory that he couldn't even remember his own name. He committed suicide the day after his 36th shock treatment.

Reference:
(http://edition.cnn.com/fyi/school.tools/profiles/hemingway/index.story.html)

656.

The visual design of Ursula from "The Little Mermaid" was based on the drag queen Divine, who was a star of the cult classic film "Pink Flamingos."

Reference:
(https://en.wikipedia.org/wiki/Ursula_(character)#Personality_and_design)

657.

At the 1992 Winter Olympics, NFL star Herschel Walker competed in the 2-man bobsled competition.

Reference:
(https://en.wikipedia.org/wiki/Herschel_Walker#Track_and_field)

658.

Immediately after giving his famous "We shall fight on the beaches" speech, Winston Churchill allegedly muttered, "And we'll fight them with the butt ends of broken beer bottles because that's bloody well all we've got!"

Reference:
(https://en.wikipedia.org/wiki/We_shall_fight_on_the_beaches#Reception)

659.

Royal Navy ships entering the Port of London are still required by law to give a barrel of rum to the Constable of the Tower.

Reference:
(http://news.bbc.co.uk/2/hi/uk_news/england/london/4527223.stm)

660.

The Powerpuff Girls was originally called "Whoopass Stew!", which featured a "can of whoopass" instead of "Chemical X".

Reference: (http://en.wikipedia.org/wiki/The_Powerpuff_Girls)

661.

"The Widower" is a dish from Grantham made with 20 infinity chilies and claimed to be the world's hottest curry. Only one person has even finished it and he took an hour, spending 10 minutes of that time hallucinating due to the endorphin rush.

Reference: (https://en.wikipedia.org/wiki/Infinity_chili)

662.

In Mississippi, it's a misdemeanor to ridicule a person who refuses to duel.

Reference: (http://law.justia.com/codes/mississippi/2013/title-97/chapter-39/section-97-39-7)

663.

Scientists in the South Pole have a tradition of sitting in a sauna and then running outside naked to the ceremonial pole and back. They can go from a 200 degrees Fahrenheit sauna to -100 degrees

Fahrenheit outside. They have to do it quickly enough otherwise they will get frostbite.

Reference:
(http://uk.mobile.reuters.com/article/idUKN1341483220061213)

664.

The House of Commons in London has a free snuff box filled with tobacco, as smoking in the chamber has been forbidden since the 1700s.

Reference: (http://www.bbc.com/news/uk-politics-24713932)

665.

There are single celled organisms that can grow up to four inches in diameter at the bottom of the world's oceans.

Reference: (http://en.wikipedia.org/wiki/Unicellular_organism)

666.

Substituting a number for a letter is called "Leetspeak" or "L337".

Reference: (http://www.robertecker.com/hp/research/leet-converter.php)

667.

A sheep named Chris that was found roaming near Canberra, Australia, had so much overgrown wool that it was difficult for him to move and see. His five year growth was sheared, producing 90 pounds of merino wool, shattering the old record of 63 pounds.

Reference: (http://www.nydailynews.com/news/world/lost-australian-sheep-shorn-89-pounds-wool-article-1.2347773)

668.

The Polish Ambassador to Iraq survived a roadside bombing in 2007. In 2010, the same man was assigned to be the Polish Ambassador to North Korea.

Reference: (https://en.wikipedia.org/wiki/Edward_Pietrzyk)

669.

When a group of U.S. tanks crossed the border into Iraq, they had a hummer with loudspeakers following them playing "Ride of the Valkyries."

Reference: (http://www.dailymotion.com/video/x1objo1_greatest-tank-battles-the-battle-of-73-easting-military-history-war-documentary_tv?start=315)

670.

22 United States veterans commit suicide every day.

Reference: (http://time.com/3694053/veteran-suicide/)

671.

Millennials are less likely to buy e-books than any other generation.

Reference: (http://www.thebookseller.com/news/millennials-least-likely-buy-e-books-304601)

672.

Mastering just 3,000 words in English will make you able to understand around 95% of common texts.

Reference: (http://www.lingholic.com/how-many-words-do-i-need-to-know-the-955-rule-in-language-learning-part-2/)

673.

The closest living relative to the bear is a pinniped, of more commonly known as the seal.

Reference:(https://en.wikipedia.org/w/index.php?title=Bear&mobile action=toggle_view_desktop)

674.

A British soldier escaped and got back into a POW camp more than 200 times without detection because of a love affair with the German daughter of the director of the marble quarry attached to the camp.

Reference: (http://www.telegraph.co.uk/news/obituaries/military-obituaries/army-obituaries/7223148/Horace-Greasley.html)

675.

75% of crimes in the United States are committed by high school dropouts.

Reference:
(https://en.wikipedia.org/wiki/Education_in_the_United_States)

676.

Billy Joel did all the vocal tracks for "The Longest Time."

Reference: (https://www.youtube.com/watch?v=a_XgQhMPeEQ)

677.

Roald Amundsen was a Norwegian explorer who, in 1909, tried to be the first man to reach the North Pole, but was beaten by Robert Peary. Upon hearing of Peary's victory, Amundsen immediately mounted an expedition to the South Pole, which he became the first to reach in 1911.

Reference: (https://en.wikipedia.org/wiki/Roald_Amundsen)

678.

A city in France has the world's first short story vending machine.

Reference: (http://www.newyorker.com/books/page-turner/how-a-city-in-france-got-the-worlds-first-short-story-vending-machines)

679.

Hugh Hefner has gone nearly deaf in recent years, which may be caused by the Viagra he uses. But, he still says he would rather have sex than have his hearing.

Reference: (http://www.celebritydiagnosis.com/2011/06/viagra-making-hugh-hefner-deaf/)

680.

Airline pilots deliberately touch down hard on the runway when it's raining in order to minimize aquaplaning.

Reference: (http://travel.usatoday.com/experts/cox/story/2011-12-12/Ask-the-Captain-Sometimes-a-hard-landing-is-a-good-one/51770628/1)

681.

The University of California offers a course about the Simpson's television show and philosophy.

Reference:
(http://www.tylershores.com/thesimpsonsandphilosophy/)

682.

The Dutch law system prevents courts from reviewing formal laws on the ground of the constitution, according to Article 120.

Reference:
(http://www.dutchcivillaw.com/legislation/constitution066.htm)

683.

Christina Hendricks' agency fired her for taking the role of Joan Holloway on Mad Men.

Reference: (http://www.people.com/article/christina-hendricks-agency-dropped-mad-men)

684.

Ottoman Sultan Murad IV banned coffee, tobacco & alcohol, making consumption a capital offense. He would patrol the streets himself, personally killing offenders. Murad was a habitual drinker himself and died of cirrhosis.

Reference: (http://en.wikipedia.org/wiki/Murad_IV)

685.

Waylon Smithers from the Simpsons was black in his first visual appearance on the show.

Reference: (http://en.wikipedia.org/wiki/Waylon_Smithers)

686.

Despite the ban on smoking on planes, the FAA requires all aircraft to still be fitted with ashtrays, so that if someone does have a cigarette, it can be disposed of safely.

Reference: (http://indy100.independent.co.uk/article/the-reason-why-aeroplanes-still-have-ashtrays--Zyx7gTuKARe)

687.

Doctors induced labor to make sure that Kim Jong-Un's child was born in 2012, which marked the 100th anniversary of North Korean founder Kim Il-Sung.

Reference:
(http://english.chosun.com/site/data/html_dir/2013/03/20/2013032000
0553.html)

688.

One of the reasons Pluto isn't a planet is that many larger objects have been found, which don't qualify as planets.

Reference: (http://www.universetoday.com/13573/why-pluto-is-no-longer-a-planet/)

689.

Achernar, the 10th brightest star in the night sky, spins so fast that its width is over 1.5 times greater than its pole-to-pole diameter.

Reference: (https://en.wikipedia.org/wiki/Achernar)

690.

One of the Popes was a complete accident. In the Middle Ages, cardinals would often vote a random candidate on the first papal ballot in order to see how the other cardinals were leaning, but in 1334, this backfired when they all voted for the same person: the very surprised, Pope Benedict XII.

Reference:(http://en.wikipedia.org/wiki/Pope_Benedict_XII#Fournier.27s_accession_to_the_Papacy)

691.

In Judaism, one of the traditional steps in circumcision involved "oral suction" to draw blood away from the cut.

Reference:
(https://en.wikipedia.org/wiki/Brit_milah#Metzitzah_B.27Peh)

692.

4 hour long NFL games only have 11 minutes of actual gameplay.

Reference: (http://www.sportsgrid.com/nfl/pie-chart-actual-football-watching-nfl-game-vs-replays-commercials-etc/)

693.

NASA has data showing from 1870 to present, an average rise in sea levels of over 3 millimeters per year.

Reference: (http://climate.nasa.gov/vital-signs/sea-level/)

694.

There is a gigantic swastika made of larch trees that went unnoticed for nearly sixty years.

Reference: (http://en.wikipedia.org/wiki/Forest_swastika)

695.

A 12 year old girl was handcuffed, booked, and fingerprinted for eating French fries in a Subway.

Reference: (http://abcnews.go.com/US/story?id=94999&page=1)

696.

Marlon Brando's, considered one of the greatest actors of all time, last role before he died was in an unreleased kid's animated film where he played an old woman.

Reference:
(http://lostmedia.wikia.com/wiki/Big_Bug_Man_(Unreleased_Anim ated_Movie))

697.

Tina Turner became a citizen of Switzerland and relinquished her U.S. citizenship in 2013.

Reference:
(https://en.wikipedia.org/wiki/Tina_Turner#Residences_and_citizens hip)

698.

Each day is 54 billionths of a second longer than the one before. This means that each day is the shortest day of the rest of your life.

Reference: (http://www.radiolab.org/story/times-they-are-changin/)

699.

Children with gray hair might have a B-12 deficiency.

Reference: (http://www.drgreene.com/qa-articles/children-gray-hair/)

700.

In 2014, a woman dropped her cell phone in an open pit toilet and 2 people died attempting to retrieve the phone.

Reference:(http://www.cnet.com/news/woman-drops-cell-phone-in-toilet-two-die-in-rescue-attempt/)

701.

Ahmed Best got a Golden Razzie for voicing Jar Jar binks in Star Wars: The Phantom Menace.

Reference:
(https://en.wikipedia.org/wiki/Stigmata_(film)#Critical_response)

702.

The German name for "Jello" translates into "food of the Gods."

Reference: (https://en.wikipedia.org/wiki/G%C3%B6tterspeise)

703.

There are as many molecules in ten drops of water as there are stars in the universe.

Reference:
(http://www.npr.org/sections/krulwich/2012/09/17/161096233/which
-is-greater-the-number-of-sand-grains-on-earth-or-stars-in-the-sky)

704.

Around 1,000 homeless people live in flood tunnels under Las Vegas.

Reference: (http://en.wikipedia.org/wiki/Mole_people#Cities)

705.

There was a fire at Ohio Penitentiary that killed 322 and injured 150 inmates. Some of the guards refused to unlock the cells which led to the inmates overpowering the guards, taking their keys and rescuing other prisoners.

Reference: (http://en.wikipedia.org/wiki/Ohio_Penitentiary)

706.

An English organist named Jeremiah Clarke wanted to commit suicide but he couldn't decide whether to hang himself or drown, so he flipped a coin. The coin landed on its edge in the mud so he ended up shooting himself instead.

Reference: (https://en.wikipedia.org/wiki/Jeremiah_Clarke)

707.

The number of passenger journeys in China during the Lunar New Year period is around 2.9 billion, making it the largest human mass migration in the world.

Reference:
(http://money.cnn.com/gallery/news/economy/2013/02/07/china-
new-year-migration/)

708.

Pope Francis is an honorary Globetrotter.

Reference: (https://www.washingtonpost.com/news/morning-mix/wp/2015/05/07/meet-the-newest-harlem-globetrotter-pope-francis/)

709.

According to a study done in 1969, the United States has had the bloodiest and most violent labor history of any industrial nation in the world.

Reference:(https://en.wikipedia.org/wiki/List_of_worker_deaths_in_United_States_labor_disputes)

710.

At the age of 12 actress, Ally Sheedy, wrote a bestselling children's book called, "She was Nice to Mice."

Reference: (https://en.wikipedia.org/wiki/Ally_Sheedy)

711.

Musa I of Mali, during a pilgrimage, gave away so much gold that it devastated the local economy for a decade.

Reference:
(https://en.wikipedia.org/wiki/Musa_I_of_Mali#Islam_and_pilgrimage_to_Mecca)

712.

50% of the population of Uganda is under the age of 15.

Reference: (http://en.wikipedia.org/wiki/Demographics_of_Uganda)

713.

When people lose weight, they lose about 80% of it in the form of exhaling carbon dioxide, not from sweat or mass converted to energy or heat.

Reference:
(https://www.sciencedaily.com/releases/2014/12/141216212047.htm
)

714.

After the Space Shuttle Columbia broke apart over Texas, a human heart belonging to one of the crew members was found.

Reference:(http://en.wikipedia.org/wiki/Space_Shuttle_Columbia_di saster#Recovery_of_debris)

715.

When "That 70s Show" started, the directors required all actors to be 18 or older. Mila Kunis, 14 at the time, told the casting directors she would be 18 but did not say when. Ashton Kutcher, Kunis' boyfriend in the show, was 20 years old at that time.

Reference: (http://en.wikipedia.org/wiki/Mila_Kunis#Career)

716.

Barry Goldwater, a U.S. presidential candidate and longtime senator, was a World War II ferry pilot who flew the treacherous "hump" over the Himalayas. He was also an early proponent of the Air Force Academy, and one of the first commanders to desegregate his flying unit in the 1950s.

Reference: (https://en.wikipedia.org/wiki/Barry_Goldwater)

717.

At Texas Tech University, a prominent statue of Will Rogers on his horse, Soapsuds, sits at the main entrance to the school. The rear end of the horse is pointed at College Station, Texas, home of the rival school Texas A&M.

Reference: (http://www.ttu.edu/traditions/rogers.php)

718.

The current Pope has a degree in chemistry and used to work as a chemist.

Reference: (http://ncronline.org/blogs/ncr-today/does-pope-francis-have-masters-degree-chemistry)

719.

Planets emit sound through radio emissions.

Reference: (http://earthsky.org/space/video-for-your-ears-what-do-planets-sound-like)

720.

Phrases like, "long time no see," and "chop chop" are grammatically incorrect and originate from Chinese immigrants. These phrases may have been coined by native speakers imitating these immigrants.

Reference: (http://www.npr.org/sections/codeswitch/2014/03/09/288300303/who-first-said-long-time-no-see-and-in-which-language)

721.

Bill Gates once released mosquitoes at his presentation on malaria, stating, "There's no reason why only poor people should have the experience."

Reference: (https://www.youtube.com/watch?v=ppDWD3VwxVg)

722.

The Beatles played a demo copy of "Sgt. Pepper's Lonely Hearts Club Band" before its release at full volume from an open apartment window at 6AM. Instead of complaining, the residents opened their windows and listened, aware that they were hearing unreleased Beatles music.

Reference:(http://en.wikipedia.org/wiki/Sgt._Pepper%27s_Lonely_Hearts_Club_Band#Cover_artwork)

723.

Landmines planted on the coasts during the Falklands War accidentally created penguin sanctuaries. The penguins are too light to detonate the mines, so they live and breed safely. The sanctuaries are so popular and profitable that there are efforts to prevent removal of the mines.

Reference: (http://en.wikipedia.org/wiki/Land_mine)

724.

Aboriginal youth represent 22% of all cases in Canada's foster care, yet they account for only 3.9% of the population. Of all children in care, the percentage of aboriginal children reach 60% to 78% in some provinces.

Reference: (https://en.wikipedia.org/wiki/Foster_care_in_Canada)

725.

A father was denied access to see his premature twins in the NICU when Beyoncé and Jay-Z were having their daughter at the same time.

Reference: (http://www.nydailynews.com/new-york/blue-beyonce-special-treatment-bed-stuy-dad-jay-z-turned-lenox-hill-private-club-article-1.1002985)

726.

The Vatican Secret Archives consists of 85 kilometers of shelving and are indexed by a catalog which spans 35,000 volumes.

Reference:
(https://en.wikipedia.org/wiki/Vatican_Secret_Archives#Extent)

727.

Kurt Gerstein was a top SS Officer who secretly tried warning the Allies of the horrors he witnesses at the Nazi Death Camps. He later committed suicide after they failed to listen to him.

Reference: (https://en.wikipedia.org/wiki/Kurt_Gerstein)

728.

There is a 4,000 year old clay tablet which is a customer's letter complaining about sub-standard copper and wanting a refund.

Reference: (https://en.wikipedia.org/wiki/Complaint_tablet_to_Ea-nasir)

729.

London Cab drivers must memorize every place of interest on all 25,000 of London's roads in order to be certified as an, "All London Cab."

Reference: (http://www.nytimes.com/2014/11/10/t-magazine/london-taxi-test-knowledge.html?_r=0)

730.

In 2008, a Brazilian priest, strapped 1000 balloons to a lawn chair and sent himself up for his part in a fundraising event. A few weeks later, he was found dead at sea; this earned him a Darwin Award.

Reference: (http://darwinawards.com/darwin/darwin2008-16.html)

731.

7 stranded German soldiers low on ammo captured Belgrade in World War II by meeting the mayor and bluffing that they are part of several tank divisions.

Reference: (http://www.historynet.com/invasion-of-yugoslavia-waffen-ss-captain-fritz-klingenberg-and-the-capture-of-belgrade-during-world-war-ii.htm)

732.

In the last 53 years, 10 actors have played the role of Ronald McDonald.

Reference:
(http://mcdonalds.wikia.com/wiki/Actors_who_have_played_Ronald_McDonald)

733.

Shaggy, the musician, was a U.S. Marine.

Reference: (https://en.wikipedia.org/wiki/Shaggy_(musician))

734.

There is up to 9 trillion kilograms of ants on the Earth.

Reference: (http://en.wikipedia.org/wiki/Biomass_%28ecology%29)

735.

The oldest continually held sporting event in the United States is a jousting tournament, which is held the third Sunday of August every year in the Natural Chimneys of Virginia.

Reference:
(http://en.wikipedia.org/wiki/Mount_Solon,_Virginia#Natural_Attractions)

736.

A woman married her soulmate "Bruce", which is a baby blue Ferris Wheel. The wedding was officiated by a priest with a soundboard.

Reference: (https://www.youtube.com/watch?v=mY64l69DNQA)

737.

Georgia levied a tax on electric cars due to falling gas price that resulted in less gas tax collections.

Reference:(http://www.slate.com/articles/business/the_juice/2015/04/georgia_passes_200_electric_car_fee_why_are_states_punishing_people_for.html)

738.

In 1886, Major League Baseball pitcher Charles "Old Hoss" Radbourn became the first person to be photographed giving the middle finger.

Reference: (http://twentytwowords.com/first-known-photograph-of-someone-giving-the-finger-1886-3-pictures/)

739.

Anti - occupation Rabbis have actually volunteered to be human shields in order to defend Palestinian villages from destruction.

Reference: (http://www.haaretz.com/news/settlers-clash-with-rabbis-guarding-palestinian-olive-harvest-near-hebron-1.254901)

740.

"Inverted Spectrum" is a philosophy that states the possibility of people agreeing on the names and characteristics of certain colors, though one person is essentially seeing a totally different color. If I have an inverted spectrum, we both say we see a bright blue sky, but if you saw it through my eyes, you could be looking at a bright red or purpose or green sky. Compare to the fact that dogs are proven to have a very limited spectrum of color, humans may also be born with access to a limited or inverted spectrum, and are never aware of it.

Reference: (http://en.wikipedia.org/wiki/Inverted_spectrum)

741.

An A.I. Ethics board was established as a result of the acquisition of DeepMind Technologies by Google.

Reference: (https://en.wikipedia.org/wiki/Google_DeepMind)

742.

The Sakhalin-Hokkaido Tunnel is a proposed tunnel that would connect the Russian island of Sakhalin to the Japanese island of Hokkaido. This, along with a bridge connecting the Russian mainland to Sakhalin, would link the Japanese and European rail networks.

Reference:
(https://en.wikipedia.org/wiki/Sakhalin%E2%80%93Hokkaido_Tunnel)

743.

One of the "cures" for the Bubonic Plague was to fart in a jar and smell it.

Reference: (http://www.peashooter85.com/post/57385991045/farts-in-a-jar-how-to-cure-the-plague-in-the)

744.

Frank Sinatra's son, Frank Sinatra Jr., was kidnapped in 1963, at age of 19. At the time, it was rumored that Sinatra had arranged the kidnapping in an attempt to promulgate his son's struggling music career.

Reference: (http://southbaycompass.com/sinatra-kidnapping/)

745.

To date, the Manx language is in a process of "resurrection" after it got extinct during the late part of the 20th century. Currently, there are about 100 proficient speakers.

Reference: (http://thedockyards.com/the-history-of-the-isle-of-man/)

746.

In competitive shooting, alcohol is considered a performance enhancing drug because it can slow your heart rate and steady your nerves.

Reference: (http://www.dailynebraskan.com/sports/alcohol-banned-from-rifle-competitions/article_208d46e3-8e6f-54b4-a2d5-98aef12ab40e.html)

747.

In 2004-2005, McDonald's paid rappers to mention Big Macs in their songs and paid them $5 each time their songs got played on the radio.

Reference: (http://news.bbc.co.uk/2/hi/business/4389751.stm)

748.

Investigators found 159 tubs of undelivered mail at a postal worker's house in 2010. After 20 years at USPS, he was caught when his coworkers found his mail load in recycling bins, and his punishment was community service and probation.

Reference: (http://www.seattlepi.com/local/article/Investigators-Disgraced-mailman-caught-burying-4392117.php)

749.

Penguins swim in a style called "porpoising," and do so to avoid predators, distract prey or out of pure joy.

Reference: (http://www.onegreenplanet.org/animalsandnature/10-things-you-never-knew-about-penguins/)

750.

You can't take celery into Chelsea FC's football ground.

Reference:
(http://www.theguardian.com/football/2007/mar/16/newsstory.sport11)

751.

Female aphids give birth to live young and while they are generally wingless, can produce winged offspring if the current plant is not suitable anymore.

Reference: (http://insects.about.com/od/truebugs/fl/10-Fascinating-Facts-About-Aphids.htm)

752.

In 2002, 30 British Marines accidentally invaded Spain.

Reference:
(http://www.theguardian.com/uk/2002/feb/19/gibraltar.world)

753.

When Bob Dylan and his band performed Danny and the Juniors, "Rock and Roll Is Here to Stay", at his high school, it was so loud that his principal cut the microphone.

Reference:
(https://en.wikipedia.org/wiki/Bob_Dylan#Origins_and_musical_beginnings)

754.

70% of the UK population support the death penalty.

Reference: (http://www.ipsos-mori.com/researchpublications/researcharchive/poll.aspx?oItemId=2504)

755.

Constantinople because Istanbul because people started referring to it as "The City" and the Greek phrase for "In The City" is pronounced as "Is Tin Poli". Over time, this became known as Istanbul.

Reference: (http://nowiknow.com/star-fortress/)

756.

An asteroid is about 17 times faster than a bullet at the moment of impact.

Reference:(https://gist.githubusercontent.com/anonymous/324dff4f82e334ff3f8e7cb6d3bc59c3/raw/d50f7d78d711cf058a17806f5dfe589e2f230f5f/til.md)

757.

The producers of the Big Bang Theory didn't give Penny, a character in the show, a last name.

Reference:
(https://en.wikipedia.org/wiki/Penny_(The_Big_Bang_Theory)#Family)

758.

At the current oil extraction rate, we will run out of oil reserves by 2070.

Reference:
(https://en.wikipedia.org/wiki/Oil_reserves#Estimated_reserves_by_country)

759.

There was a dinosaur with fingers like swords.

Reference:
(http://en.wikipedia.org/wiki/Therizinosaurus#Description)

760.

The Bank of England has issued a number of £100,000,000 bank notes, known as "Titans", which never leave the vault.

Reference:(http://en.wikipedia.org/wiki/Bank_of_England_note_issues#.C2.A31.2C000.2C000_and_.C2.A3100.2C000.2C000)

761.

Cribbing involved a horse grabbing a solid object with its incisors, then arching its neck, pulling against the object and sucking in air. This releases endorphins in the horse's brain, getting it high. It's also very addictive.

Reference: (https://en.wikipedia.org/wiki/Cribbing_(horse))

762.

The mysterious Black Knight Satellite is actually just a thermal blanket let go from the ISS.

Reference: (https://en.wikipedia.org/wiki/Black_Knight_satellite)

763.

Peyton Manning yells "Omaha" before a play to either switch the direction of a play or to confuse the defensive line with extra meaningless calls.

Reference: (http://www.sbnation.com/nfl/2014/2/2/5371134/peyton-manning-omaha-super-bowl-48)

764.

A chimpanzee named Frodo has impregnated his own mother, killed a human infant, attacked cartoonist Gary Larson, and beat the head of primatology, Jane Goodall, so badly that he almost broke her neck.

Reference:
(http://en.wikipedia.org/wiki/Kasakela_Chimpanzee_Community#Frodo)

765.

According to the New York Business Journal, the Campbell Soup Co. has recently dramatically increased its marketing budget with the launch of a multimedia ad campaign centered around a boy with a long beard, "The Wisest Kid in the Whole World", who advises people to have soup.

Reference:
(http://www.bizjournals.com/newyork/news/2013/09/10/campbell-soups-new-ads-aimed-at.html?page=all)

766.

The Gompertz-Makeham Law of Mortality states that your chance of dying in any given year doubles every 8 years.

Reference:
(https://en.wikipedia.org/wiki/Gompertz%E2%80%93Makeham_law_of_mortality)

767.

During the 2008 world hops shortage, the Samuel Adams brewery shared 20,000 pounds of their excess hops with 108 different craft breweries, at cost, to help prevent them from going out of business.

Reference:(http://en.wikipedia.org/w/index.php?title=Samuel_Adams_%28beer%29#2008_hops_shortage)

768.

The infamous Pinkerton Company, known as violent strike busters during the 1800s and early 1900s, is still in business today as a security guard and detective agency.

Reference:
(https://en.wikipedia.org/wiki/Pinkerton_(detective_agency))

769.

David Bowie's 1983 hit, "Let's Dance," featured and helped to launch the career of the future guitar legend, Stevie Ray Vaughan.

Reference:
(https://en.wikipedia.org/wiki/Let%27s_Dance_(David_Bowie_album))

770.

In the movie "Babe", 48 real piglets were used. Piglets grow very quickly and all the pigs used in the movie were female because the male genitalia would have been too obvious on screen.

Reference: (http://www.ew.com/article/1995/08/18/real-pigs-steal-scene-babe)

771.

The famous science fiction thriller "Primer" was created on a $7,000 dollar budget. Shane Carruth acted as the main character, writer, director, producer, cinematographer, editor and sole music composer. He worked on post-production for two years and almost abandoned the project many times.

Reference: (https://en.wikipedia.org/wiki/Primer_(film)#Production)

772.

Modern football is descended from medieval football. It was played between neighboring towns and villages, involving an unlimited number of players on opposing teams, who would attempt to bring an inflated pig's bladder to markers at each end of a town.

Reference: (https://en.wikipedia.org/wiki/Medieval_football)

773.

Daisy Ridley's great uncle played the lovable Private Godfrey on Dads Army.

Reference: (https://en.wikipedia.org/wiki/Arnold_Ridley)

774.

The photographer of the Pulitzer Prize winning photo depicting a vulture waiting for a starving child to die, committed suicide due to guilt, persecution and depression.

Reference: (http://en.wikipedia.org/wiki/Kevin_Carter)

775.

12.5 million Africans were shipped to the Americas and sold into slavery. However, only 388,000 ended up in the United States.

Reference:(http://www.theroot.com/articles/history/2012/10/how_many_slaves_came_to_america_fact_vs_fiction.html)

776.

Ludwig van Beethoven was dragged from his bed to play the keyboard when he was a little kid.

Reference:
(https://en.wikipedia.org/wiki/Ludwig_van_Beethoven#Background_and_early_life)

777.

Octopoteuthis deletron break off their own arms to throw at predators, allowing it to jet away to safety.

Reference: (https://en.wikipedia.org/wiki/Octopoteuthis_deletron)

778.

The preservation of the gene pool of the Ukrainian people is the duty of the State. This was mandated in response to the Chernobyl disaster.

Reference: (http://faolex.fao.org/cgi-bin/faolex.exe?rec_id=127467&database=faolex&search_type=link &table=result&lang=eng&format_name=@ERALL)

779.

The screams of those being gassed during the Holocaust were so disturbing that in order to stifle them, SS Officers would rev motorcycles as far as they would go. This proved to be futile, so they built gas chambers offsite.

Reference: (http://www.pbs.org/auschwitz/40-45/orders/1941b.html)

780.

The FBI recruited a Mafia enforcer to use "illegal interrogation techniques" on members of the KKK in order to find the bodies of three missing civil rights workers. The techniques worked.

Reference:
(http://en.wikipedia.org/wiki/Gregory_Scarpa#Mississippi_civil_rig hts_workers)

781.

Haikus aren't simply 5-7-5 syllable poems, but also need to have a "kigo", which is something of or relating to a season.

Reference:
(http://teacher.scholastic.com/LessonPlans/pdf/dec05_unit/whatishaiku.pdf)

782.

The Mars Climate Orbiter Mission failed as the result of one team programming the landing based on the English system of measurement while other teams programmed it expecting the metric system to be used.

Reference: (https://en.wikipedia.org/wiki/Mars_Climate_Orbiter)

783.

In the 19th Century, Americans purposely filled their parks with squirrels for entertainment purposes. They were rarely found outside of the forest beforehand.

Reference: (http://gizmodo.com/the-fascinating-story-of-why-u-s-parks-are-full-of-squ-1478182563)

784.

Because of the isolated location and frigid climate, Antarctica, Greenland, Iceland, some of Polynesia and the Hawaiian Islands are believed to have no native ant species.

Reference:
(http://en.wikipedia.org/wiki/Ant#Distribution_and_diversity)

785.

That the engraving, "Do Not Duplicate", on some keys is merely a suggestion and can be legally duplicated by locksmiths.

Reference:
(http://en.wikipedia.org/wiki/Key_(lock)#Do_not_duplicate_key)

786.

Eye cells are deactivated in the presence of light to allow for its perception.

Reference:
(http://www.acbrown.com/neuro/Lectures/NrVisn/NrVisnRtnlHprp.htm)

787.

2008 had the second largest Youth Voter turnout in United States history, mainly due to the Facebook Effect.

Reference: (http://facebook.about.com/od/Advanced/tp/6-Ways-Facebook-Has-Changed-Politics.htm)

788.

"Soft drinks" are called "soft" in contrast to "hard drinks", which are drinks with more than 0.5% alcohol by volume.

Reference: (https://en.wikipedia.org/wiki/Soft_drink)

789.

Emperor Nero dressed up a slave boy as the wife he'd had killed and called him by her name.

Reference: (https://en.wikipedia.org/wiki/Sporus)

790.

An "ultracrepidarian" is somebody who gives opinions on subjects they know nothing about.

Reference: (http://en.wikipedia.org/wiki/Ultracrepidarianism)

791.

Thomas Edison offered Nikola Tesla $50,000 to improve his DC motor. Upon completion, Edison failed to pay and scoffed, "You don't understand American humor."

Reference: (http://www.history.com/topics/inventions/nikola-tesla)

792.

There was a real team of Jewish assassins who called themselves "the Avengers" who organized after World War II to track down and execute Nazi war criminals.

Reference: (http://en.wikipedia.org/wiki/Nakam)

793.

An Ohio man called police in a panic because he thought that he had smoked too much marijuana. The police found him in a fetal position, surrounded by Doritos, Pepperidge Farm Goldfish, and Chips Ahoy Cookies. The man was fine, and the police didn't charge him with any crime.

Reference: (http://www.vindy.com/news/2015/oct/05/man-too-high-marijuana-calls-austintown-police-hel/)

794.

In the original Snow White story, instead of sharing a tender kiss with her fair prince, Snow White vomited up the poisoned apple.

Reference: (http://www.goodreads.com/story/show/60644-the-true-origins-and-history-of-snow-white-and-the-seven-dwarfs)

795.

An Ohio man called police in a panic because he thought that he had smoked too much marijuana. The police found him in a fetal position, surrounded by Doritos, Pepperidge Farm Goldfish, and Chips Ahoy Cookies. The man was fine, and the police didn't charge him with any crime.

Reference: (http://www.vindy.com/news/2015/oct/05/man-too-high-marijuana-calls-austintown-police-hel/)

796.

Batman voice actor Kevin Conroy roomed with Robin Williams while at Julliard.

Reference: (https://en.wikipedia.org/wiki/Kevin_Conroy#Personal_life)

797.

In 1888, a pigeon fancier and a beekeeper challenged each other's creatures to a 3.5 mile organized race in Germany. The bee won by 25 seconds.

Reference: (http://www.bbc.com/news/blogs-magazine-monitor-28546844)

798.

Pyongyang, in North Korea, has an International Film Festival.

Reference: (https://en.wikipedia.org/wiki/Pyongyang_International_Film_Festival)

799.

President Hoover invented Hooverball, a volleyball like game that's played with a 10 pound medicine ball.

Reference: (https://en.wikipedia.org/wiki/Hooverball)

800.

More people die from champagne corks than from poisonous spiders.

Reference:
(http://www.scientificcomputing.com/articles/2009/07/do-we-really-understand-risks)

801.

A migrant is a person who moves from one place to another within a country, while an immigrant is a person who moves from one country to another.

Reference: (http://www.modbee.com/opinion/letters-to-the-editor/article33660813.html)

802.

Cockroaches experience performance anxiety. A study found that cockroaches running through a hard maze will have more difficulties if other roaches are watching them.

Reference:
(http://en.wikipedia.org/wiki/Social_facilitation#Activation_theory)

803.

American pediatrician, Saul Krugman, participated in deliberately infecting thousands of mentally disabled children with Hepatitis A and B between the 1950s and 1970s to further his research in vaccinology. He was later made the President of the American Pediatric Society in 1972.

Reference: (http://ahrp.org/1955-1970-saul-krugman-md-conducted-despicable-medical-experiments-at-willowbrook/)

804.

In 2013, Oxford researcher Kevin Dutton compiled a list of professions that attract the most psychopaths. It probably won't come as a surprise that plenty of psychopaths become police officers, lawyers and surgeons. However, the number one vocation chosen by psychopaths was CEO.

Reference: (http://listverse.com/2014/03/20/10-crazy-facts-about-psychopaths/)

805.

The reason why announcers and commentators of the 1950s spoke so oddly was because they spoke something called "Transatlantic Speech". The other reason why was because the audio receivers of the day couldn't pick up bass tones.

Reference: (http://news.discovery.com/history/us-history/old-time-baseball-players-talk-130404.htm)

806.

Muhammad Ali managed to talk a suicidal man out of jumping to his death after police and psychologists had failed.

Reference: (https://www.youtube.com/watch?v=SV75aFzC1aQ)

807.

There is a cognitive bias called the Google effect where a person tends to forget information that can easily be found using a search engine.

Reference: (http://en.wikipedia.org/wiki/Google_effect)

808.

Bugs don't breathe or have lungs. They have a network of tubes where air flows and oxygen is simply absorbed.

Reference: (https://askabiologist.asu.edu/how-insects-breathe)

809.

Hugh Laurie from the television show, "House", is also one of the main characters in the British sitcom, "Blackadder."

Reference: (https://en.wikipedia.org/wiki/George_(Blackadder))

810.

It is entirely possible for a chicken to lay an egg that contains another fully developed egg.

Reference:
(http://www.todayifoundout.com/index.php/2015/02/possible-chicken-egg-within-chicken-egg/)

811.

The "Baby on Board" stickers often seen on cars are made by a highway safety association. They are to notify other drivers to be cautious around that vehicle.

Reference: (https://en.wikipedia.org/wiki/Baby_on_board)

812.

The Stanley Cup was established in 1892 by the Governor General of Canada, Lord Stanley of Preston, and isn't actually owned by the NHL and can even possibly be awarded to teams outside of the NHL.

Reference: (https://thenib.com/meet-the-stanley-cup-704c3c5a39c8#.w5wl2ow3h)

813.

Bee stings contain a compound called isopentyl acetate that attracts other bees to join an attack. Isopentyl acetate is also the compound that provides the scent of bananas.

Reference: (http://www.mainebee.com/articles/beestings.php)

814.

On the night of September 2nd, 1859, a conversation lasting two hours was held between telegraph operators in Portland, Maine and Boston using only current generated by the Aurora Borealis.

Reference:
(http://en.wikipedia.org/wiki/Aurora#Auroral_events_of_historical_significance)

815.

Cherophobia is the fear of being too happy because "something tragic" will happen.

Reference: (http://en.wikipedia.org/wiki/Aversion_to_happiness)

816.

The Ocean Quahog is a clam that doesn't appear to age. One specimen has been confirmed to be over 500 years old.

Reference:
(https://en.wikipedia.org/wiki/Arctica_islandica#Longevity)

817.

Matthew Todd Miller travelled to North Korea intending to get arrested, claiming that he was a computer hacker involved with WikiLeaks. He was sentenced to six years of forced labor, but was released 2 months later.

Reference: (https://en.wikipedia.org/wiki/Matthew_Todd_Miller)

818.

Despite billions of pounds worth being printed and used every year, there is no legal tender paper money in Scotland. In fact, even Scottish bank notes are not legal tender in Scotland.

Reference:(https://en.wikipedia.org/wiki/Banknotes_of_the_pound_sterling#The_question_of_legal_tender)

819.

There's a salmon cannon, designed by a company called Whooshh Innovations.

Reference: (http://www.theverge.com/2014/8/11/5983681/whooshh-innovations-wants-to-whooshh-your-fish-to-safety)

820.

After "I Am Legend" was finished, Will Smith developed such a bond for the German Shepard that he tried to buy it from the owner.

Reference: (http://www.today.com/id/22264942/ns/today-today_entertainment/t/will-smith-falls-love-legend-co-star/)

821.

Denmark has the oldest flag in the world that's still in use, with the current design adopted before 1370.

Reference:(https://en.wikipedia.org/wiki/List_of_sovereign_states_by_date_of_current_flag_adoption)

822.

The term "basket case" originated from incapacitated quadruple amputees needing to be carried around in baskets after World War I.

Reference: (http://blog.oxforddictionaries.com/2015/06/9-words-with-offensive-origins/)

823.

The U.S. Navy shot down a civilian airliner that was on route to Dubai from Tehran in 1988, killing 290 people, in Iranian airspace and waters.

Reference: (https://en.wikipedia.org/wiki/Iran_Air_Flight_655)

824.

Saudi Arabia uses 52% of its energy on air conditioning in the summer peaks.

Reference:(https://www.chathamhouse.org/sites/files/chathamhouse/public/Research/Energy,%20Environment%20and%20Development/1211pr_lahn_stevens.pdf)

825.

Airplanes are legally required to have ashtrays and can be grounded without them.

Reference: (http://gizmodo.com/5912352/why-airplanes-still-have-ashtrays-in-the-bathrooms)

826.

The Former U.S. Secretary of State, political scientist and novel price winner, Henry Kissinger, was quoted with saying, "military men are dumb, stupid animals to be used as pawns for foreign policy." He never denied saying that.

Reference: (http://www.phibetaiota.net/2013/06/henry-kissinger-military-men-are-dumb-stupid-animals-to-be-used-as-pawns-for-foreign-policy/)

827.

Whites used to pay to throw balls at blacks at the circus. They were called "African Dodgers".

Reference:
(http://www.ferris.edu/news/jimcrow/question/oct12/index.htm)

828.

Crocodiles and dinosaurs are more closely related to birds than reptiles.

Reference: (https://en.wikipedia.org/wiki/Feathered_dinosaur)

829.

San Alfonso del Mar is a resort in Chile that houses the world's largest swimming pool. The pool is 1 kilometer long and holds 250 million gallons of water.

Reference: (https://en.wikipedia.org/wiki/San_Alfonso_del_Mar)

830.

Mailing an entire building has been illegal in the U.S. since 1916 when a man mailed a 40,000 ton brick house across Utah to avoid high freight rates.

Reference: (http://web.archive.org/web/20120331044805/http://www.postalmuseum.si.edu/exhibits/2b2f_parcel.html)

831.

There is a leper colony on a Hawaiian island with patients still there.

Reference:
(http://www.thedailybeast.com/articles/2015/08/30/hawaii-still-has-a-leprosy-colony-with-six-patients.html)

832.

Sweden pays high school students $187 per month to attend school.

Reference:
(http://www.csn.se/en/2.1034/2.1036/2.1037/2.1038/1.9265)

833.

A 63 year old man named Edward Smith is a mechaphile and has had sex with over 700 cars.

Reference: (http://www.mirror.co.uk/tv/tv-news/man-who-sex-over-700-4435804)

834.

Putting dry tea bags in smelly shoes or gym bags will absorb the unpleasant odor.

Reference: (http://greatist.com/health/treat-sunburns-tea-and-other-tips)

835.

The man who wrote Microsoft Word and invented the red squiggly for misspellings is now a professional poker player.

Reference: (http://www.idgconnect.com/abstract/8829/meet-man-who-wrote-microsoft-word)

836.

Two men were brought up on federal hacking charges when they exploited a bug in video poker machines and won half a million dollars. Their lawyer argued, "All these guys did is simply push a sequence of buttons that they were legally entitled to push." The case was dismissed.

Reference: (http://www.wired.com/2013/11/video-poker-case/)

837.

According to new research, psychopaths don't lack empathy, rather they can switch it on and off at will.

Reference: (http://www.bbc.com/news/science-environment-23431793)

838.

Lee Harvey Oswald's corpse was exhumed in the early 1980's because there was a widely believed conspiracy theory that the body actually belonged to a Russian spy who had assumed his identity in order to kill John F. Kennedy. Tests concluded, however, that the body was in fact Oswald's.

Reference: (http://www.nytimes.com/1981/10/05/us/oswald-s-body-is-exhumed-an-autopsy-affirms-identity.html)

839.

The Cheyenne Chief Black Kettle, a major advocate for peace and coexistence between white settlers and Native Americans, was twice attacked by American troops despite explicit agreement of non-hostility, resulting in the death and mutilation of him and at least two hundred Cheyenne villagers.

Reference:
(http://www.pbs.org/weta/thewest/people/a_c/blackkettle.htm)

840.

You need a license to dance in Sweden.

Reference: (http://www.thelocal.se/20120921/43380)

841.

The Greek national anthem has 158 verses.

Reference:(https://el.wikisource.org/wiki/%CE%8E%CE%BC%CE%BD%CE%BF%CF%82_%CE%B5%CE%B9%CF%82_%CF%84%CE%B7%CE%BD_%CE%95%CE%BB%CE%B5%CF%85%CE%B8%CE%B5%CF%81%CE%AF%CE%B1%CE%BD)

842.

In 1996, when a man was arrested for wearing a Medal of Honor he did not earn, a judge forced him to write an apology letter to all living Medal of Honor recipients as punishment.

Reference: (http://en.wikipedia.org/wiki/Medal_of_Honor)

843.

The first ever World Series of Poker Champion to qualify through an online poker site has "Moneymaker" as a legitimate family name. His ancestors were German coin minters who anglicized the name from "Nurmacher."

Reference: (https://en.wikipedia.org/wiki/Chris_Moneymaker)

844.

Japan Airlines require all staff to visit a museum dedicated to the JAL flight 123 disaster of August, 1985, when 520 people lost their lives.

Reference: (http://www.bbc.co.uk/news/magazine-33931693)

845.

Only one tenth of the money raised from the Hurricane Sandy relief concert was actually donated to relief funds.

Reference:
(http://www.foxnews.com/entertainment/2013/10/29/celebs-raised-millions-fo-sandy-relief-so-where-did-it-go/)

846.

The United States gave Mexico $420 million dollars in aid in 2013.

Reference:
(https://en.wikipedia.org/wiki/United_States_foreign_aid#Recipients
)

847.

Parts of speech, such as verbs and nouns, were first used in Sanskrit literature.

Reference: (https://en.wikipedia.org/wiki/Part_of_speech#India)

848.

Heather Graham's parents forbid her from being in the movie "Heathers" because the script had too many expletives.

Reference: (https://en.wikipedia.org/wiki/Heather_Graham)

849.

Segway was bought out by a Chinese company known as Ninebot, which was founded years after Segway and specialized in a knock off version of the Segway.

Reference: (http://nextshark.com/chinese-segway-knock-off-company-buys-out-real-segway-company/)

850.

Brad Pitt found his acting coach through strippers.

Reference: (https://www.youtube.com/watch?v=cFfarLUWjpo&feature=youtu.be&t=419)

851.

Eric Burdon, lead singer of the Animals, claims to be the "Eggman" mentioned in the song "Am the Walrus" due to his fondness of breaking eggs over naked women's bodies.

Reference: (https://en.wikipedia.org/wiki/I_Am_the_Walrus)

852.

From 1934 to 1962, the United States Government subsidized $120 billion dollars in home loans, of which 98% went to white families.

Reference: (http://www.pbs.org/race/000_About/002_06_a-godeeper.htm)

853.

The reason so many Spanish names end in "ez," is because "ez" means "descendant of."

Reference: (http://blog.dictionary.com/last-name-ends-in-ez/)

854.

Cows orient themselves to magnetic north.

Reference:
(http://www.scientificamerican.com/article.cfm?id=cattle-deer-sense-magnetic-field)

855.

A 19 year old man dove 85 feet into the ocean to wrestle an 80 pound octopus with a 9 foot diameter to the surface. The battle lasted 25 minutes, in which he punched the octopus to subdue it before it turned red and lunged at him, tearing off his respirator. Eventually the man managed to kill the octopus, drive it home, cook it and eat it.

Reference: (http://www.nytimes.com/2013/10/20/magazine/the-octopus-that-almost-ate-seattle.html?_r=0)

856.

There is an ancient temple in Ireland that predates Giza and Stonehenge. During the winter solstice, light penetrates through to the burial tomb for about 19 minutes.

Reference: (http://newgrange.com/)

857.

The actor who played Spartacus in the original movie in 1960, Kirk Douglas, is still alive at the age of 99.

Reference: (https://en.wikipedia.org/wiki/Kirk_Douglas)

858.

Illegal coal mining activities in Mongolia, and the intense use of coal burned on simple stoves has turned a region of Mongolia, once famed for its blue skies, into one of the worlds most polluted regions.

Reference:
(http://www.worldcoal.com/coal/02042014/Illegal_coal_mining_in_Mongolia_683/)

859.

The serial killer with the most victims – possibly over 400 – was only sentenced to 30 years in jail.

Reference: (http://en.wikipedia.org/wiki/Luis_Garavito#Sentencing)

860.

The Bloodhound Project will try to break the land speed world record by reaching 1000 MPH this year in Africa with their rocket powered car.

Reference: (http://qnr.ca/video-2/rocket-powered-car/)

861.

The Soviets tried to cross breed apes and humans.

Reference:
(https://en.wikipedia.org/wiki/Ilya_Ivanovich_Ivanov#Human-ape_hybridization_experiments)

862.

Henry Ford attempted to create a utopian society that was free from time clocks, malaria and caterpillars. He planned for the society to be located in the Amazon and called it Fordlandia.

Reference: (https://en.wikipedia.org/wiki/Fordl%C3%A2ndia)

863.

There have actually been more than 400 earthquakes in Nepal since the first one struck exactly one year ago.

Reference: (http://earthquakes.possiblehealth.org/)

864.

The "Miss Cleo free tarot reading" psychic hotline was generating $24 million a month for two years straight. Miss Cleo herself only earned $1,750 for the three days it took to film the first infomercial.

Reference: (http://www.vice.com/read/we-spoke-to-ms-cleo-about-her-fake-patois-and-getting-ripped-off-by-her-old-bosses)

865.

The average amount of time a woman can keep a secret is 47 hours and 15 minutes.

Reference:
(http://www.telegraph.co.uk/news/newstopics/howaboutthat/6199822/Women-cannot-keep-a-secret-for-longer-than-47-hours.html)

866.

Dolphins like to get high off a neurotoxin released by a particular species of pufferfish.

Reference: (https://www.youtube.com/watch?v=msx3BAhIeQg)

867.

You can travel by train from Singapore to London for $2,126.

Reference: (https://vulcanpost.com/2150/he-travelled-from-singapore-to-london-across-14-countries-by-land-it-only-costs-us2126/)

868.

As of 2010, over 17% of the United States population lives on less than 2% of the country's land area, in what is known as the Northeast Megalopolis.

Reference: (https://en.wikipedia.org/wiki/Northeast_megalopolis)

869.

A sheep named Chris that was found roaming near Canberra, Australia, had so much overgrown wool that it was difficult for him to move and see. His five year growth was sheared, producing 90 pounds of merino wool, shattering the old record of 63 pounds.

Reference: (http://www.nydailynews.com/news/world/lost-australian-sheep-shorn-89-pounds-wool-article-1.2347773)

870.

The United States is responsible for 62% of worldwide sales of any new medicine.

Reference:
(http://www.efpia.eu/uploads/Figures_Key_Data_2013.pdf)

871.

A severed snake head can still bite you, hours after the snake has been dead.

Reference: (http://www.livescience.com/47626-severed-snake-head-can-still-bite.html)

872.

Between 1977 and 1978, Ethiopia and Somalia, both of which were communist at the time, fought a massive tank war in the Osgaden Dessert. The USSR, East Germany, North Korea, Cuba and South

Yemen backed Ethiopia while China and Romania supported Somalia in one of the most bizarre wars of the 20th century.

Reference:
(https://en.wikipedia.org/wiki/Ogaden_War#Course_of_the_war)

873.

People who smoke have almost 50% lower risk of Parkinson's Disease.

Reference: (http://www.neurologyadvisor.com/movement-disorders/parkinsons-disease-smoking-nicotine-tobacco-use-neuroprotective/article/458995/)

874.

In 2004-2005, McDonald's paid rappers to mention Big Macs in their songs and paid them $5 each time their songs got played on the radio.

Reference: (http://news.bbc.co.uk/2/hi/business/4389751.stm)

875.

The founder of Kodak, George Eastman, killed himself because he had accomplished everything that he felt necessary to do and didn't feel like waiting for his diabetes to kill him slowly.

Reference: (http://www.biography.com/people/george-eastman-9283428)

876.

A horror movie known as "Playback" cost $7.5 million dollars to produce, but earned only $264 after having only one showing.

Reference: (https://en.wikipedia.org/wiki/Playback_(film))

877.

An 18th century astronomer went to India to see a Transit of Venus. Delayed, he missed it, but decided to stay for the next one, which occurred in 8 years. The second try was clouded out so 3 years later, he returned home. When he came back to France, he found that he had been declared dead, his wife had remarried and his estate was gone.

Reference: (http://messier.seds.org/xtra/Bios/legentil.html)

878.

People who have damage to their brain's amygdala nuclei regions, such as from the rare Urbach–Wiethe disease, are unable to experience the emotion of fear.

Reference:
(https://en.wikipedia.org/wiki/Fear#Inability_to_experience)

879.

Whites used to pay to throw balls at blacks at the circus. They were called "African Dodgers".

Reference:
(http://www.ferris.edu/news/jimcrow/question/oct12/index.htm)

880.

There was a French "invasion" on British soil. In 1998, the Minquiers, a small group of islands in the English Channel, was invaded by 7 French men on behalf of the "King of Patagonia" in retaliation for the British occupation of the Falkland Islands. The Union Jack was restored the next day.

Reference: (http://news.bbc.co.uk/2/hi/uk_news/162190.stm)

881.

If it were a country, California would be the 8th biggest economy in the world and the 35th most populous country in the world.

Reference: (http://www.latimes.com/business/la-fi-california-world-economy-20150702-story.html)

882.

There are over 10 million Manchu people but only about 10 left who still speak the Manchu language.

Reference: (https://en.wikipedia.org/wiki/Manchu_people)

883.

Natalie Portman and Danica McKellar are among the 15 lowest Erdos-Bacon-Sabbath numbers on Earth.

Reference: (http://timeblimp.com/?page_id=195)

884.

There's a set of biracial twins in the UK who are turning heads because one is black and the other is white.

Reference: (http://nypost.com/2015/03/02/meet-the-bi-racial-twins-no-one-believes-are-sisters/)

885.

Norwegian explorer and writer, Thor Heyerdahl, stated that ancient people from South America could have settled in Polynesia, but most anthropologists didn't believe him. So, in 1947, he built a primitive raft and made the 101 day journey himself.

Reference: (http://en.wikipedia.org/wiki/Kon-Tiki)

886.

A British soldier escaped and got back into a POW camp more than 200 times without detection because of a love affair with the German daughter of the director of the marble quarry attached to the camp.

Reference: (http://www.telegraph.co.uk/news/obituaries/military-obituaries/army-obituaries/7223148/Horace-Greasley.html)

887.

The stereotypical nonchalance of Italian men is called "Sprezzatura."

Reference: (https://en.wikipedia.org/wiki/Sprezzatura?1)

888.

During Liechtenstein's last military deployment, they sent 80 soldiers. When they returned, they had 81 men, as they befriended an Italian during the deployment.

Reference: (http://media.lonelyplanet.com/shop/pdfs/2143-Switzerland_-_Liechtenstein__Chapter_.pdf)

889.

A book titled, "The Pink Swastika," makes the claim that many Nazi leaders, including Hitler, were homosexual. Though historians label the work as, "utterly false," and have thoroughly discredited it, the book is still frequently cited when discussing LGBT rights.

Reference: (https://en.wikipedia.org/wiki/The_Pink_Swastika)

890.

There is a species of large centipedes native to Texas that can grow up to 8 inches. They feast on lizards, toads, rodents and snakes.

Reference: (http://www.mnn.com/earth-matters/animals/stories/giant-snake-eating-centipede-spotted-texas)

891.

Mike Todd is the only one of Elizabeth Taylor's seven husbands whom she didn't divorce.

Reference: (https://en.wikipedia.org/wiki/Mike_Todd)

892.

In Iceland, belief in elves is still prevalent enough to hinder building projects. In December of 2013, Elf Advocates urged the Icelandic Road and Coastal Commission to abandon a highway project for fear of disturbing an elf habitat that includes an elf church.

Reference: (http://www.mercurynews.com/bay-area-living/ci_24783212/could-there-be-elves-iceland)

893.

The actor who played "Tone" in the 1991 movie "Point Break" was once the lead singer of a music band called The Red Hot Chili Peppers.

Reference: (http://www.nydailynews.com/entertainment/point-break-cast-gallery-1.2237870?pmSlide=1.2237864)

894.

Japanese swordsmiths are limited to making 24 per year, which is one of the reasons they cost so much.

Reference: (http://en.wikipedia.org/wiki/Shinken)

895.

In Japanese mythology, the Japanese archipelago was created by an Amenonuhoko, a "heavenly jeweled spear", which was dipped into the sea.

Reference: (http://www.ancient-mythology.com/japanese/izangi-izanami.php)

896.

The flower, "forget me nots," were used by freemasons during the Nazi reign to remember the poor and desperate so as not to be singled out and persecuted.

Reference: (https://en.wikipedia.org/wiki/Forget-me-not)

897.

Native Americans have the highest interracial marriage rate among all single race groups in the United States.

Reference: (https://en.wikipedia.org/wiki/Interracial_marriage)

898.

Purple isn't a real color. It's just something our brains make up to rationalize a lack of green photons.

Reference: (https://youtu.be/iPPYGJjKVco)

899.

It's possible to "scrub" carbon dioxide out of the air. The captured CO2 can then be used to create low-carbon fuels or stored to eliminate the emissions from the atmosphere.

Reference:
(http://www.canadianmanufacturing.com/technology/canadian-firm-builds-giant-scrubber-to-pull-co2-from-the-air-152497/)

900.

A billionaire on house arrest in Florida was allowed to charter a plane and fly himself and his guards to Texas to see his ailing mother.

Reference: (http://www.chron.com/news/houston-texas/houston/article/Billionaire-John-Goodman-allowed-private-jet-trip-4743708.php)

901.

The more expensive the car, the more likely the driver is to cut off pedestrians and other cars on the road.

Reference: (http://articles.latimes.com/2012/feb/27/science/la-sci-0228-greed-20120228)

902.

There's a set of biracial twins in the U.K. who are turning heads because one is black and the other is white.

Reference: (http://nypost.com/2015/03/02/meet-the-bi-racial-twins-no-one-believes-are-sisters/)

903.

A company in Japan offers a "baby bonus" of $400 for the first child and up to $40,000 for the fifth child.

Reference: (https://en.wikipedia.org/wiki/SoftBank#Baby_bonus)

904.

$44 billion worth of gift cards have gone unredeemed since 2008.

Reference: (http://nypost.com/2014/01/26/unused-gift-cards-total-44b-since-2008-study/)

905.

Texan public school students are required to pledge allegiance to the state flag instead of the United States flag.

Reference:
(http://www.statutes.legis.state.tx.us/Docs/ED/htm/ED.25.htm#25.08
2)

906.

2 F16 pilots went on a suicide mission to stop Flight 93 on 9/11.

Reference: (http://www.washingtonpost.com/local/f-16-pilot-was-ready-to-give-her-life-on-sept-11/2011/09/06/gIQAMpcODK_story.html)

907.

More Americans live in Mexico City than Wyoming.

Reference: (http://en.wikipedia.org/wiki/Mexico_City#Geography)

908.

In 1973, the crew of Skylab 4 staged the first strike in space. They requested time off to look out the window and think.

Reference:
(http://www.nytimes.com/2014/03/11/science/space/william-r-pogue-astronaut-who-flew-longest-skylab-mission-is-dead-at-84.html?_r=2)

909.

In 1955, the United States Government dropped over 300,000 mosquitoes over the state of Georgia for research purposes.

Reference: (https://en.wikipedia.org/wiki/Operation_Big_Buzz)

910.

Historically, Chinese doctors only got paid if their patients were healthy. Payment would stop if the patient got sick, until the health returned.

Reference: (http://seqclinic.com/chinese_medicine.html)

911.

In 1872, an Englishman posing as Lord Gordon-Gordon swindled $1 million from a rail magnate and almost caused a battle between the United States and Canada.

Reference: (https://en.wikipedia.org/wiki/Lord_Gordon_Gordon)

912.

The World Health Organization classed shift work as a carcinogenic in 2007.

Reference:
(http://www.webmd.com/cancer/news/20071130/night_shift-work-may-cause-cancer)

913.

The movie "Who Framed Roger Rabbit," was based on a book called "Who Censored Roger Rabbit," and they have very little in common.

Reference: (http://www.avclub.com/article/book-vs-film-iwho-framed-roger-rabbiti-8568)

914.

Norway knighted a penguin.

Reference:
(http://www.edinburghzoo.org.uk/animals/SirNilsOlav.html)

915.

In 1965, Nick Nolte was sentenced for selling counterfeit documents and was given a 45 year jail sentence and a $75,000 fine. However, the sentence has since been "temporarily" suspended.

Reference: (https://en.wikipedia.org/wiki/Nick_Nolte#Personal_life)

916.

A man faked mental illness to escape jail, was sent to an asylum and has been trying since to convince doctors that he's sane. He's been diagnosed as a psychopath because in part, "faking mental illness to get out of a prison sentence is exactly the kind of manipulative act you would expect of a psychopath."

Reference: (http://blogs.wsj.com/ideas-market/2011/05/23/pretending-to-be-crazy%E2%80%94all-too-effectively/)

917.

In 2007, an angry moose attacked a helicopter in Alaska.

Reference: (http://www.foxnews.com/story/2007/03/07/angry-moose-brings-down-helicopter-in-alaska.html)

918.

Scouting Honey Bees perform a dance when they get back to the hive to direct other bees to sources of food. The bees provides distance and direction using the sun as a reference point.

Reference: (https://en.wikipedia.org/wiki/Waggle_dance)

919.

Fornication between unmarried, consenting individuals is a Class 4 Misdemeanor in Virginia.

Reference: (https://vacode.org/18.2-344/)

920.

Approximately 1 in 3 people are millionaires in Monaco.

Reference: (http://www.ibtimes.co.uk/one-three-people-monaco-millionaire-1458415)

921.

The Draughtsboard shark can bark like a dog when it's stressed.

Reference: (http://www.elasmo-research.org/education/topics/b_sounds.htm)

922.

A study by an American University found that the Toyota Camry and the Honda Accord both contain more domestic content than the "American" Chevrolet Camaro.

Reference: (http://www.carsdirect.com/automotive-news/cities-that-drive-the-most--and-least--american-cars)

923.

When the Russian submarine, Kursk, sank in the Bering Sea with 118 sailors on board, Russia turned down offers from Britain and Norway to send a rescue mission, saying that the crew had been killed by an explosion. The bodies of 24 initial survivors were found in a compartment 9 days later.

Reference:
(https://en.wikipedia.org/wiki/Russian_submarine_Kursk_(K-141)#Rescue_attempts)

924.

Steve, from the popular kids show "Blue's Clues", once surprised a child by randomly showing up to his Blue's Clues themed birthday party while he was on a date with a Playboy model.

Reference:
(https://www.youtube.com/watch?v=CwmtkFPYXsg&feature=iv&src_vid=BMw1-KOMxRI&annotation_id=annotation_750247)

925.

A man in Taiwan was mauled by a lion after he jumped into their enclosure with a bible in an attempt to convert them to Christianity.

Reference: (http://articles.latimes.com/2004/nov/04/world/fg-lion4)

926.

The extreme temperatures of Mt. Everest can freeze the lungs and cause a cough so violent, it can tear chest muscles and break ribs. It's known as the Khumbu Cough.

Reference: (http://www.climbing-high.com/khumbu-cough.html)

927.

There was a fifth, female Teenage Mutant Ninja Turtle named Venus de Milo.

Reference: (https://en.wikipedia.org/wiki/Venus_(Teenage_Mutant_Ninja_Turtles))

928.

Michael Jordan's number 23 was retired by the Miami Heat, even though he never played for the Heat.

Reference: (http://mentalfloss.com/article/29246/11-jersey-numbers-retired-unconventional-reasons)

929.

The first African American drafter by an NFL team was George Taliaferro. In college, at Indiana University, he led the team in rushing, passing and putting at various points in his career.

Reference: (https://en.wikipedia.org/wiki/George_Taliaferro)

930.

Memorial Day originated as Decoration Day after the American Civil War in 1868, as a time for the nation to decorate the graves of those who died in the war with flowers.

Reference: (http://en.m.wikipedia.org/wiki/Memorial_Day)

931.

The song "Cherry Bomb", by the Runaways, only reached number 106 on the American charts but number 1 in Japan and Scandinavia.

Reference:
(https://en.wikipedia.org/wiki/Cherry_Bomb_(The_Runaways_song)
)

932.

A B-29 bomber from World War II was found abandoned in Greenland. In 1995, an effort to recover the bomber failed when the plane caught fire during the first takeoff attempt, leaving the plane in shambles. It still lies where it has for over 60 years.

Reference: (https://en.wikipedia.org/wiki/Kee_Bird)

933.

Thousands of microscopic mites live on your face.

Reference: (http://www.bbc.com/earth/story/20150508-these-mites-live-on-your-face)

934.

It's impossible to sneeze in your sleep.

Reference:
(http://en.wikipedia.org/wiki/Sneeze#Overall_mechanism)

935.

There once was a village named Resia in Italy. They flooded the area and the only thing left visible is the village's bell tower. It is now known as Lago di Resia.

Reference: (http://en.wikipedia.org/wiki/Reschensee)

936.

A woman woke up at her own funeral and was so shocked by it that she had a heart attack and died.

Reference: (http://unusualdeaths.com/2012/06/01/fagilyu-mukhametzyanov/)

937.

Bats don't flap their entire forelimbs, as birds do, but instead flap their spread out digits.

Reference: (https://en.wikipedia.org/wiki/Digit_(anatomy))

938.

Itai-itai disease, which translates to the "It hurts, it hurts" disease, is caused by poisoning from cadmium pollution in Japan.

Reference: (https://en.wikipedia.org/wiki/Itai-itai_disease)

939.

As a result of a 20 year old online joke that the German city of Bielefeld doesn't actually exist, the city released a press statement titled "There Really is a Bielefeld!". However, as it was released on April 1st, this just added to the conspiracy.

Reference: (http://en.wikipedia.org/wiki/Bielefeld_Conspiracy)

940.

The commander at Pearl Harbor on December 7th, 1941, was such a creature of habit that the Japanese Military read his tactics easily. His fault habitualness also gave him confidence that Japan could never attack Pearl Harbor first. He was relieved of his duties 10 days later.

Reference: (http://www.history.com/this-day-in-history/commander-at-pearl-harbor-canned)

941.

James Frey, who is notorious for the "A Million Little Pieces" controversy, is Pittacus Lore, the author of the book "I Am Number Four."

Reference: (https://en.wikipedia.org/wiki/James_Frey)

942.

The Green Bay Packers are the only non-profit, community owned major league professional sports team based in the United States.

Reference: (https://en.wikipedia.org/wiki/Green_Bay_Packers,_Inc.)

943.

For 12 days during the Battle of Berlin in World War II, a group of 770, 50 year old World War I veterans in the Bolkssturm militia held their district against the approaching Soviet army until they had just 26 rifles and 2 light machine guns left. 26 of them were awarded the Iron Cross.

Reference:
(https://en.wikipedia.org/wiki/Volkssturm#Battle_for_Berlin)

944.

The hinged arms on glasses are actually called "skull temples."

Reference: (http://optometristattic.com/temples.htm#Skull)

945.

After dropping in on a performance of his play, "Of Thee I Sing," George S. Kaufman was so unhappy with one of the actors that he left the theatre and immediately sent him a telegram saying, "Watching your performance from the last row. Wish you were here."

Reference: (http://www.delanceyplace.com/view_sresults.php?1230)

946.

It's illegal to handle salmon under "suspicious circumstances" in the United Kingdom due to the 1986 Salmon Law.

Reference: (http://www.legislation.gov.uk/ukpga/1986/62/contents)

947.

There is a company that provides private flights for individuals who want to join the "mile high club." For $425 you get a 1 hour flight, chocolates, champagne, and a curtain.

Reference: (http://www.maxim.com/maxim-man/art-seduction/article/flamingo-air%E2%80%99s-flights-fancy-new-mile-high-club)

948.

Multiple sclerosis is an unpredictable disease that effects nearly 2.5 million people worldwide, with about 200 new cases every week in just the United States alone.

Reference: (http://main.nationalmssociety.org/goto/decker_austin)

949.

The Persian Sufi saint, Bayazid Bastami, was once presented with a watermelon, and he refused to eat it because he couldn't be certain that Prophet Muhammad had ever eaten one.

Reference: (https://en.wikipedia.org/wiki/Sufism#Prophet_Muhammad)

950.

A Las Vegas mental hospital used commercial busses to "dump" more than 1,500 psychiatric patients in 48 states over five years.

Reference: (http://www.pulitzer.org/citation/2014-Investigative-Reporting)

951.

Raffles Station was built to work as a bombing shelter. It was originally made to house 200 to 300 people for 3 days, but now it can hold thousands.

Reference: (http://eresources.nlb.gov.sg/infopedia/articles/SIP_864_2004-12-30.html)

952.

Over 12.8 million U.S. adults, which is about 5.2% of the population, have a concealed handgun permit.

Reference: (http://crimeresearch.org/2015/07/new-study-over-12-8-concealed-handgun-permits-last-year-saw-by-far-the-largest-increase-ever-in-the-number-of-permits/)

953.

Bank of America bought Countrywide Financial in 2008 for $2.5 billion and by 2014 the deal had already generated $50 billion in losses for Bank of America.

Reference: (http://www.charlotteobserver.com/news/business/banking/article9151889.html)

954.

Jupiter's moon, Europa, has more water than Earth. Its subsurface ocean plus ice layer could range from 80 to 170 kilometers in average depth.

Reference: (http://apod.nasa.gov/apod/ap120524.html)

955.

Former NFL hall of famer, Mike Webster, bought himself a taser gun, used it on himself to treat his back pain, and would sometimes zap himself into unconsciousness just to get some sleep.

Reference: (http://www.gq.com/sports/profiles/200909/nfl-players-brain-dementia-study-memory-concussions/)

956.

London only reached its pre-World World II population level in January, 2015.

Reference: (http://www.citymetric.com/skylines/week-when-londons-population-will-finally-overtake-its-previous-peak-606)

957.

Over 12.8 million U.S. adults, which is about 5.2% of the population, have a concealed handgun permit.

Reference: (http://crimeresearch.org/2015/07/new-study-over-12-8-concealed-handgun-permits-last-year-saw-by-far-the-largest-increase-ever-in-the-number-of-permits/)

958.

Living animals were put on the Bikini Atoll atomic bomb test site for research information.

Reference: (https://youtu.be/jYUP7zJ0CwU?t=497)

959.

Art critics unknowingly believed chimp paintings to be incredible modern art.

Reference: (http://en.wikipedia.org/wiki/Pierre_Brassau)

960.

An indoor vegetable factory in Japan produces up to 10,000 heads of lettuce per day and uses just 1% of the amount of water needed for outdoor fields.

Reference: (http://www.gereports.com/post/91250246340/lettuce-see-the-future-japanese-farmer-builds)

961.

There's an increase in time wasting searches the day after Daylight Savings Time starts and people aren't doing anything at work.

Reference: (http://www.rawstory.com/2015/03/how-daylight-savings-time-impacts-your-health/)

962.

Four teenage girls lied to have an innocent man convicted of murdering a child. After they were found out, they never apologized, claiming that they did it "for a laugh".

Reference: (https://en.wikipedia.org/wiki/Murder_of_Lesley_Molseed)

963.

Tracie Ruiz, the Olympian, won the 1984 Olympic gold medal for solo synchronized swimming.

Reference: (https://en.wikipedia.org/wiki/Tracie_Ruiz)

964.

There is a frog in Africa, Trichobatrachus Robustus, which breaks a bone in its toe pad, pushes the sharp broken bone through its skin and tries to stab you with it if it feels threatened.

Reference: (http://www.newscientist.com/article/dn13991-horror-frog-breaks-own-bones-to-produce-claws.html#.VDCIgPldXh5)

965.

Steven Spielberg said that Robert Shaw was so drunk during the first shooting of his famous USS Indianapolis speech in "Jaws" that he couldn't even complete it. When he woke from his blackout, Shaw called Spielberg to apologize and begged him to re-shoot the scene. He was ready at 7:30AM the next morning.

Reference: (http://www.aintitcool.com/node/49921)

966.

Hugh Hefner has gone nearly deaf in recent years, which may be caused by the Viagra he uses. But, he still says he would rather have sex than have his hearing.

Reference: (http://www.celebritydiagnosis.com/2011/06/viagra-making-hugh-hefner-deaf/)

967.

In the 18th century, it was common to literally blow smoke up someone's rectum for resuscitation and to treat a variety of medical conditions.

Reference: (http://www.historyextra.com/qa/smoke-it-out)

968.

Elle King, singer of "Ex's and Oh's," is Rob Schneider's daughter.

Reference: (http://www.billboard.com/articles/news/magazine-feature/6753770/elle-king-breakout-hit-exs-and-ohs-dad-rob-schneider-wild-child)

969.

Tom Hanks kicked the Fonz through a window on one episode of "Happy Days."

Reference: (https://www.youtube.com/watch?v=lA_hNoGDM4Y)

970.

Prisons across the United States serve certain inmates a one-dish meal called "nutriloaf," which was specifically designed to be bland, flavorless, and unappealing.

Reference: (http://www.chicagomag.com/Chicago-Magazine/September-2010/Dining-Critic-Tries-Nutraloaf-the-Prison-Food-for-Misbehaving-Inmates/)

971.

There is an offshoot of straightedge subculture called hardline, which opposes drug use, eating meat, and any type of sex that isn't for the sake of procreation; this includes homosexuality and masturbation.

Reference:
(https://en.wikipedia.org/wiki/Hardline_%28subculture%29)

972.

In the Netherlands, heroin addicts are given free heroin at clinics three times a day. Some addicts complain that the government makes being an addict too easy for an individual, but overall heroin addiction has decreased.

Reference: (https://news.vice.com/article/only-in-the-netherlands-do-addicts-complain-about-free-government-heroin)

973.

Many tattoo artists refuse to put neck and face tattoos on lightly or non-tattooed customers.

Reference: (http://www.huffingtonpost.com/lori-leven/heres-what-i-have-to-say-_b_7701856.html)

974.

In World War II, J.F.K. saved a man, after their boat was sunk, by swimming three miles to a nearby island, all while towing the man by his life-preserver's strap, with his teeth.

Reference: (http://www.history.navy.mil/faqs/faq60-2.htm)

975.

In 2011, a pair of managers from Dominos set fire to a Papa John's restaurant in order to boost their sales.

Reference:
(http://archive.firstcoastnews.com/topstories/article/224762/483/Dominos-Managers-Arrested-in-Papa-Johns-Pizza-Arson)

976.

All the coconuts of the world can be traced to two very distinct genetic varieties. One of them is from the Pacific Ocean in South East Asia, and the other is from the Indian Ocean in Southern India.

Reference: (https://source.wustl.edu/2011/06/deep-history-of-coconuts-decoded/)

977.

The United States Navy has 3,700 aircraft, making it the second largest air force in the world.

Reference: (http://nationalinterest.org/feature/the-five-most-powerful-navies-the-planet-10610)

978.

Tim Tebow was predicted as being stillborn.

Reference: (http://www.webcitation.org/6C3RRbZ4e)

979.

The first air - to - air combat attempts were made by throwing bricks and grenades from plane to plane during World War I.

Reference:
(http://www.sparknotes.com/history/european/ww1/section5.rhtml)

980.

Praying mantis are the only insects that can turn their head side to side 180 degrees.

Reference: (http://www.bugfacts.net/praying-mantis.php)

981.

A bidet is considered a key green technology and uses significantly less water, electricity, and wood than a single roll of toilet paper.

Reference: (http://www.scientificamerican.com/article/earth-talks-bidets/)

982.

A book titled, "The Pink Swastika," makes the claim that many Nazi leaders, including Hitler, were homosexual. Though historians label the work as, "utterly false," and have thoroughly discredited it, the book is still frequently cited when discussing LGBT rights.

Reference: (https://en.wikipedia.org/wiki/The_Pink_Swastika)

983.

While it's illegal to place weapons of mass destruction on any celestial body, it's perfectly legal to place "conventional weapons" in space.

Reference: (https://en.wikipedia.org/wiki/Outer_Space_Treaty)

984.

George Lazenby wasn't an actual actor. He got himself a suit, a Rolex and a new haircut, then met with the producer and made up movies he had been in. He later landed the role of James Bond.

Reference: (https://www.moviezine.se/video_collections/everything-or-nothing-the-untold-story-of-007-george-lazenby-om-007)

985.

The Aboriginal Mbabaram word for dog is "dog". This type of coincidence is called a "false cognate" and there are many occurrences throughout the world.

Reference: (http://en.wikipedia.org/wiki/False_cognate)

986.

Firefighters would hide in Ground Zero rubble so that dogs could find "survivors." Constantly finding bodies was leading to high stress in the dogs as they thought they were failing.

Reference: (http://www.wbur.org/2011/09/07/sept-11-search-dogs)

987.

The original surveyors of Mount Everest lied and added 2 feet to its height to make it 29,002 feet, because they didn't think people would believe them if they said it was really 29,000 feet high.

Reference:
(http://climbing.about.com//od/mountainclimbing/a/EverestFacts.htm)

988.

There was a project in the 1960s that aimed to drill a hole through the Earth's crust.

Reference: (https://en.wikipedia.org/wiki/Project_Mohole)

989.

Ines Ramirez Perez is the only woman documented to have performed a caesarean section on herself and survive, alongside her child.

Reference:
(http://www.smh.com.au/articles/2004/06/01/1086037758224.html)

990.

Johnny Depp is in a band called Hollywood Vampires.

Reference:
(https://en.wikipedia.org/wiki/Hollywood_Vampires_(band))

991.

Joni Mitchell started smoking at the age of 9, but she claims that it hasn't affected her voice.

Reference: (https://en.wikipedia.org/wiki/Joni_Mitchell#Early_life)

992.

Tadamichi Kuribayashi was the Lieutenant General who led the defensive against the United States on Iwo Jima for 36 days in the face of overwhelming odds with tactics unorthodox to the Imperial Army. For a while before the war, he lived in the United States and even studied at Harvard.

Reference: (https://en.wikipedia.org/wiki/Tadamichi_Kuribayashi)

993.

The white athlete in the famous 1968 Olympics Black Power Salute picture, Peter Norman, had his career ruined and was treated like an outsider upon returning to Australia.

Reference: (http://www.altgaze.com/?p=2426)

994.

In 1982, the CIA worked with Canadians to give Soviet spies intentionally flawed software for a natural gas pipeline. "The result was the most monumental non-nuclear explosion and fire ever seen from space."

Reference:
(http://en.wikipedia.org/wiki/Siberian_pipeline_sabotage)

995.

The average age of the scientists who worked on the Manhattan Project was 25 years old.

Reference:
(http://www.nytimes.com/2006/10/06/us/06project.html?_r=1&)

996.

A man named Set Putnam wrote a song about how being in a coma was stupid, and soon after went into a coma himself. After he awoke, when asked how it felt to be in a coma he said, "It was just as fucking stupid as I wrote about in my song."

Reference: (http://en.wikipedia.org/wiki/Seth_Putnam)

997.

The dates between October 4th, 1582 and October 15th, 1582 don't exist. 10 days were skipped when the Gregorian calendar was implemented to resolve discrepancies between the solar year and the Julian calendar.

Reference:
(https://en.wikipedia.org/wiki/Gregorian_calendar#Preparation)

998.

John Harington, the inventor of the toilet, is an ancestor of Kit Harington, who plays Jon Snow in the television show "Game Of Thrones".

Reference: (http://www.thewrap.com/game-thrones-star-kit-harrington/)

999.

The Earth's shape is called an oblate spheroid.

Reference: (https://en.wikipedia.org/wiki/Figure_of_the_Earth)

1000.

According to one researcher, ancients such as Alexander the Great were sometimes buried in honey. After about a hundred years, candied corpses were supposedly dug up and eaten as medicine.

Reference:
(http://www.npr.org/templates/story/story.php?storyId=129024911)

www.ingramcontent.com/pod-product-compliance
Lightning Source LLC
Chambersburg PA
CBHW051254250726

48656CB00004B/1294